THE DEMONS IN THE EKUR

Angels, Demons, Plasmas, Patristics, and Pyramids

JOSEPH P. FARRELL

Adventures Unlimited Press

Other Books by Joseph P. Farrell:

The Giza Death Sar Revisited
Hess and the Penguins
Hidden Finance
The Third Way
Nazi International
Thrice Great Hermetica and the Janus Age
Covert Wars and the Clash of Civilizations
Saucers, Swastikas and Psyops
Covert Wars and Breakaway Civilizations
LBJ and the Conspiracy to Kill Kennedy
Roswell and the Reich
Reich of the Black Sun
The S.S. Brotherhood of the Bell
Babylon's Banksters
The Philosopher's Stone
The Vipers of Venice
Secrets of the Unified Field
The Cosmic War
The Giza Death Star
The Giza Death Star Deployed
The Giza Death Star Destroyed
Transhumanism (with Scott deHart)
The Grid of the Gods (with Scott deHart)

THE DEMON IN THE EKUR

Angels, Demons, Plasmas, Patristics, and Pyramids

The Demon in the Ekur

by Joseph P. Farrell

ISBN:978-1-948803-64-9

Published by:
Adventures Unlimited Press
One Adventure Place
Kempton, Illinois 60946 USA

auphq@frontiernet.net

www.adventuresunlimitedpress.com

Cover by Joe Boyer

10 9 8 7 6 5 4 3 2 1

THE DEMON IN THE EKUR

Angels, Demons, Plasmas, Patristics, and Pyramids

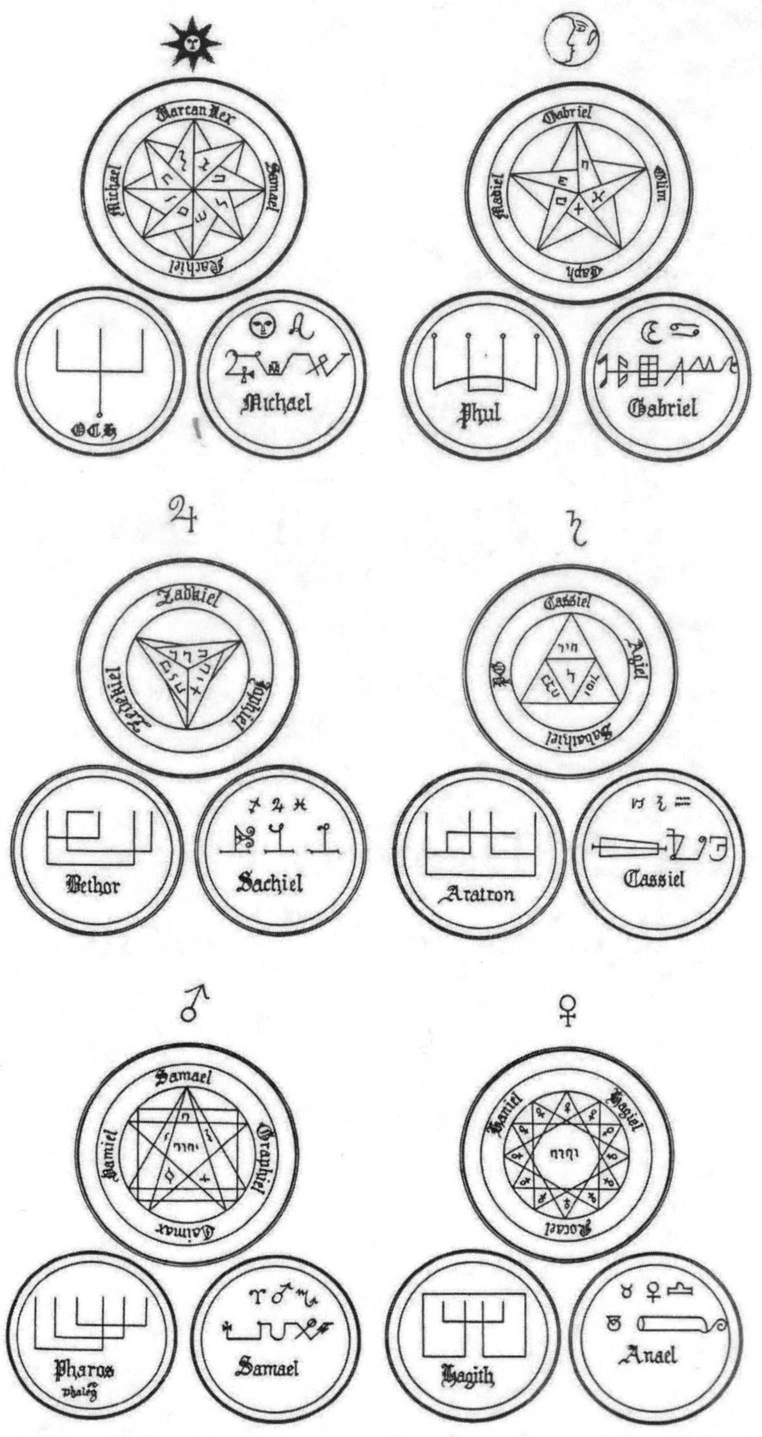

Marcan Rex
Samael
Michael
OCH
Michael
Gabriel
Phul
Gabriel
Zadkiel
Bethor
Sachiel
Cassiel
Agiel
Aratron
Cassiel
Samael
Graphiel
Pharos
Samael
Haniel
Hagiel
Hagith
Anael

Table of Contents

To all who were there at the beginning of this journey – to T.S.F.,
P.H., and M.T. Cohen –
and those who joined it along the way:
all the "Gizars" who have made the trip
and the conversation so enjoyable,
this little book is dedicated with profound gratitude.

1
INTRODUCTION: "WHAT IF...?"

"The heavens declare the glory of God; and the firmament showeth his handy-work.
One day telleth another; and one night certifieth another.
There is neither speech nor language; but their voices are heard among them.
Their sound is gone out into all lands; and their words into the ends of the world."
Psalm 19: 1-4, Coverdale edition.[1]

"Helix-shaped plasma crystals, which may be a form of so-called 'weird life,' could potentially be found in the rings of Saturn."
Jacob Silverman[2]

THIS MAY WELL BE THE STRANGEST BOOK of high speculation I have ever written, for it is prompted by my attempt to relate two seemingly disparate things: (1) the "weapon hypothesis" of the Great Pyramid, and (2) the emerging hypothesis that the vast plasmas and "dust clouds" of interstellar and intergalactic space may represent enormous and little understood life forms, life forms that by their very nature are both inorganic, "bodiless," and almost immaterial in nature. What prompted this attempt was a "connecting link" between the two complex hypotheses, a link that I call simply "The Demon in the *ekur*." As I detailed in my book *The Cosmic War*, the Akkadian term *ekur* forms a complex of concepts, meaning both "mountain" or "planet," but also

[1] Psalm 19:1-4, Coverdal edition, *The Book of Common Prayer*, 1928 edition, Protestant Episcopal Church (New York: Seabury Press, 1953), p. 363.

[2] Jacob Silverman, "Are we looking for aliens in the wrong places?" https://science.howstuffworks.com/weird-life.htm.

"ziggurant" or "pyramid." Thus, "the Demon in the *ekur"* can also be understood to be "the Demon in the pyramid." With the one stroke of this connecting link, the relationship of demons and gods with pyramidal structures is rationalized. In any case, like the "weapon hypothesis" of the Great Pyramid itself, the notion of "the Demon in the *ekur*/pyramid" is not my own. It is, once again, Zechariah Sitchin's, and a bit of discussion of that concept is in order to explain why I am only writing about it *now*, and did not do so twenty-some years ago when I first attempted to flesh out the weapon hypothesis in *The Giza Death Star* trilogy of books, or more recently, with their "update" in *The Giza Death Star Revisited.*

To come immediately to the point, I knew about "the Demon in the *ekur*/pyramid" when I first wrote *The Giza Death Star* over twenty years ago. As I pointed out in the introduction to *that* book, even *it* is not the original version of the book. The original version *did* include Sitchin's reference to "the Demon in the *ekur*," but as I also pointed out in the original introduction, as the publisher to whom I originally submitted the book was deliberating on whether or not to publish it, I continued to "crunch numbers," and to my relief, that publisher rejected the book, which allowed me to re-write the book with the newly-crunched numbers, and to submit it to another publisher, which turned out to be Adventures Unlimited Press and its owner-publisher, David Hatcher Childress, who *did* publish the book which became *The Giza Death Star* in its publicly extant text.[3]

In that resubmitted and revised manuscript, however, I *removed* Sitchin's reference to "the Demon in the *ekur*" for two reasons: firstly, the reference would have required a *much* more speculative development and would have

[3] See my *Giza Death Star* (Kempton, Illinois: 2001), pp. i-ii, and the Corvis Press Reprint (Lulu, 2022), pp. i-ii.

obscured the weapon hypothesis even more, and secondly, *while such development certainly would modify the weapon hypothesis considerably, it was not absolutely required for its articulation.* In other words, the weapon hypothesis does not stand or fall if the implications of "the Demon in the *ekur*" are true or not. The only thing "the Demon in the *ekur*" does is to modify certain aspects of the weapon hypothesis in a particular direction and in a particular way. I therefore opted to remove the reference, and decided to *hint* at its potential development and elaboration via my repeated references to the plasma cosmology of Swedish plasma physicist Hannes Alfvèn and American plasma physicist Anthony Peratt in my book *The Cosmic War*.

When I decided to re-issue the original *Giza Death Star* trilogy of books and to attempt a new summary of their argument in *The Giza Death Star Revisited*, I restored the Sitchin quotation epigraph that referred to "the Demon in the *ekur*" in that fourth book, with every intention of doing a webinar on that precise subject in the members' area of my website. Again, my reason for restoring the quotation in that work was because, by this point, certain areas of speculation in plasma physics had grown to the point that the most radical of its suggestions—that some vast interstellar and inter-galactic plasmas might be alive and even intelligent—had gained enough traction that other people were seriously beginning to entertain and write about the idea, making it possible for me to indulge in speculation about what the implications of this idea might be for cosmology in general and the Great Pyramid-as-weapon-of-mass-destruction in particular.

To put all this in the clearest possible terms, in this book we are concerned with the relationship of three conceptual complexes:

(1) That the Great Pyramid was intended as, built to be, and used as, a weapon of mass destruction;
(2) That plasma—the most abundant form of matter in the universe by far—may constitute a form of "inorganic life" and moreover, a form of potentially vast (a) extension, (b) age, (c) intellect, and therefore (d) power; and finally,
(3) That there is a definite relationship between the above two concepts that may explain much concerning both ancient weapons of mass destruction and the wars of the Gods in the textual record. Indeed, in those ancient texts, the gods and their weapons are oftentimes difficult to distinguish, and the hypotheses of plasma life rationalizes this datum rather neatly.

But why bother with such a highly speculative modification of what is already a highly speculative and radical hypothesis, namely, that the Great Pyramid was a tremendously powerful weapon? Why complicate that with a *much* more radical hypothesis that some plasmas may actually be not only alive, but intelligent, conscious, and of vast extension, age, memory, and antiquity?

The answer to those questions may be obtained by breaking them down into more detailed "What if…?" questions, each indicating the direction of the speculative hypotheses advanced later in this book. For convenience's sake, each question or series of questions is numbered, and corresponds to their number in the subsequent pages of this book:

1) What if life is the fundamental constituent of the cosmos, and not a tiny fraction of it? What if it is fundamental, and not the exception?

2) What constitutes life? What makes an organism? Is entanglement a fundamental feature of life, consciousness, and intelligence?

3) What if there are some people who think that interplanetary, interstellar, and intergalactic dusty plasmas are inorganic life forms?

4) What if they are intelligent life forms? What does their vast expanse and age say about their memory, intelligence, and power?

5) Does their nearly immaterial state constitute a rational and scientific basis for the ancient view of angels and demons as "bodiless" powers? Does it rationalize the ancient view shared by Neoplatonic, Gnostic, and other schools that there is a super-fine and almost immaterial matter that is "less dense" than ordinary matter?

6) Does this less dense state account for nineteenth century physics' view that there is a super-fine *aether lumeniferous* that is the conductive medium of electromagnetic waves?

7) Would a hypothesis of "inorganic plasma life" explain the ancient view that science, religion, and philosophy all overlap and are much more profoundly unified than modern thinking allows? Does such a view explain such ideas as morphogenetic fields, astral or "bardo" bodies? Does it explain the ancient view of the universe as a meta-organism and not a machine? Does it explain the ancient view that man is a microcosm, or for that matter, the view of St. Maximus the Confessor that the universe is a "macanthropos" or "macro-man"? Does it explain or rationalize such phenomena as "astral bodies" and "projection"? Might it explain or account for such phenomena as remote viewing, sensing, clairvoyance, clairaudience, and so on?

8) And what might all of this have to do with the Weapon Hypothesis of the Great Pyramid?

Upon careful consideration, all of these questions, with perhaps but the exception of the eighth and last, reveal themselves to be but implications of what happens when one assumes that some plasmas—even those of vast extent and age—might be some form of inorganic, intelligent, bodiless life. These questions, in other words, can be restated as propositions in a thesis abstract.

This indeed is the approach taken in the following pages. The propositions are far from proven, nor would many scientists nor even metaphysicians, nor theologians, agree with them. Our purpose is thus not to *prove* them, but rather to examine what happens when one assumes that they are true. Needless to say, assuming that they are true also does not mean that they are universally true and that all plasmas *are* "inorganic life forms," only that some may be, and if so, what the truly vast and extraordinary implications may be.

But before we examine all that, we must first take a look at "the Demon in the Pyramid"…

An Artistic Representation of a "Throne," and of Ezekiel's Vision. Note the small man at the bottom of the picture

An artistic representation of a Seraph, the bringer and keeper of fire

2
THE DEMON IN THE *EKUR*/PYRAMID

"Gravitation alone cannot separate an initially symmetric ambiplamsa (containing equal quantities of matter and antimatter) into matter and antimatter. However, in principle, this is possible under the action of electromagnetic effects."
—Hannes Alfvén[1]

A. Sts. Dionysius and John of Damascus on Angels
1. Dionysius' Celestial Hierarchies

THROUGHOUT HUMAN HISTORY, AND SCATTERED throughout innumerable texts and lore from across the globe, there are traditions concerning the incorporeal powers and intelligences, living beings—though bodiless and typically invisible—of great power, intelligence, and tremendous focused intention for good or evil that we commonly call angels and demons. There is also a great deal of unanimity among these traditions as to the specific capabilities of such entities. They can heal, or cause illness; they appear to be able to go through solid walls or windows, yet paradoxically, can also appear to certain people and at certain times to possess solid bodies; they can appear and disappear at will; they can in their demonic form possess both man and beast, causing them to behave abnormally and insanely. In some traditions these entities are also given charge over various worlds or planets, or even some regions or nations on Earth, and presumably, whole regions of the heavens, and not just particular planets. Such concepts imply a kind of "celestial hierarchy" of angels and demons, and

---

[1] Hannes Alfvén, *Cosmic Plasma*, Astrophysics and Space Science Library, Volume82 (Dordrecht, Holland: D. Reidel Publishing Company, 1981), p. 102.

indeed, the individual calling himself by the name of the Christian saint, Dionysius the Areopagite, wrote a treatise on angelology titled precisely *The Celestial Hierarchies*, a blend of biblical angelological terminology of cherubim, seraphim, principalities, powers, thrones, dominations, archangels and finally, lowly plain, ordinary angels, all neatly arranged into a nice and conveniently Neoplatonic "Ennead," a three-by-three matrix of nine types of angels, as follows:

1) In the first rank: *Seraphim, Cherubim, and Thrones;*
2) In the second or middle rank: *Dominions, Powers, and Authorities;*
3) In the third or last rank: *Principalities, Archangels, and Angels.*[2]

This Platonic and Neoplatonic arrangement will assume even more significance in a subsequent chapter, when we examine the basics of plasma cosmology and the hypothesis of plasma life.

2. John of Damascus' Angelology

For the moment, however, it is necessary to turn to another exposition of the celestial hierarchy of angels, that of St. John of Damascus (ca. 675-749) in his *De Fide Orthodoxa,* a work considered to be a crucial component and an essential compendium of traditional patristic Orthodox Catholic theology from the late seventh and early eighth

[2] Q.v. Pseudo Dionysius. *The Complete Works.* The Classics of Western Spirituality. Translated (from the Greek) by Colm Luibheid (New York: The Paulist Press, 1987), pp. 143-191. The question of whether these names indicate distinct *genera or species* of angels, or whether they represent merely a kind of angelic analogue to human races, is never completely resolved in angelology.

century, a work extensively cited in the Middle Ages by such theologians and luminaries as John Scotus Eriugena, Albertus Magnus, or Thomas Aquinas in the West, or Photios or Gregory Palamas in the East. What the Damascene has to say about angels and demons is rather extensive; we cite it in full, numbering and italicizing those portions that are the focus of our interest:

> CHAPTER THREE
> *Concerning Angels*
>
> He is Himself the Maker and Creator of the angels: for He brought them out of nothing into being and created them after His own image, *(1) an incorporeal race, a sort of spirit or* ***immaterial fire****:* in the words of the divine David, *He maketh His angels spirits, and His ministers a flame of fire,*[3] and he has described their lightness and the ardour, and heat, and keenness and sharpness with which they hunger for God and serve Him, and how *(2) they are borne to the regions above and are quite delivered from all material thought.*[4]*An angel, then, is an intelligent essence, in perpetual motion, with free will, incorporeal*, ministering to God, having obtained by grace *(3) an immortal nature; and the Creator alone knows the form and limitation of its essence.* But all that we can understand is, that it is *incorporeal and immaterial. (4) For all that is compared with God Who alone is incomparable,* ***we find to be dense and material****. For in reality only the Deity is immaterial and incorporeal.*
>
> The angel's nature then is rational, and intelligent, and endowed with free-will, changeable in will, or fickle. For

[3] Citing Psalm 104:4.

[4] At this point the editor and translator of the text inserts a footnote indicating that the Damascene has made reference to the fourth century Cappadocian Church Father, St. Gregory the Theologian's (Nazianzus) *Oration 38.*

all that is created is unchangeable, and only that which is uncreated is changeable. Also all that is rational is endowed with free-will. As it is, then, rational and intelligent, it is endowed with free-will; and as it is created, it is changeable, having power either *(5) to abide or progress in goodness, or to turn towards evil.*

It is not susceptible of repentance because it is incorporeal. For it is owing to the weakness of his body that man comes to have repentance.

It is immortal, not by nature but by grace. For all that has had beginning comes also to its natural end. But God alone is eternal, or rather, *(6)He is above the Eternal: for He, the Creator of times, is not under the dominion of time, but above time.*

(7) They are secondary intelligent lights derived from that first light which is without beginning, for *they have the power of illumination; they have no need of tongue or hearing, but without uttering words they communicate to each other their own thoughts and counsels.*[5]

Through the Word, therefore, all the angels were created, and through the sanctification by the Holy Spirit were they brought to perfection, sharing each in proportion to his worth and rank in brightness and grace.

(8) They are circumscribed; for when they are in the Heaven they are not on the earth: and when they are sent by God down to the earth, they do not remain in the Heaven. (9) They are not hemmed in by walls and doors, and bars and seals, for they are quite unlimited. Unlimited, I repeat, *(10) for it is not as they really are that they reveal themselves to the worthy men to whom God wishes them to appear, but in a changed form which the beholders are capable of seeing.* For that alone is naturally and strictly unlimited which is uncreated. For every created thing is limited by God Who created it.

---

[5] Q.v. Psalm 19: 1-4.

Further, apart from their essence they receive the sanctification from the Spirit: through the divine grace they prophecy: *(11) They have no need of marriage for they are immortal.*

(12) Seeing that they are minds they are in mental places,[6] *and are not circumscribed after the fashion of a body*. For they have not a bodily form by nature, *nor are they extended in three dimensions*. But to whatever post they may be assigned, there they are present after the manner of a mind and energise, *(13)* ***and cannot be present and energise in various places at the same time.***

Whether they are equals in essence or differ from one another we know not. God, their Creator, Who knoweth all things, alone knoweth. *(14) But they differ from each other in brightness and position,* whether it is that their position is dependent on their brightness, or their brightness on their position: and they impart brightness to one another, because they excel one another in rank and nature.[7] And clearly the higher share their brightness and knowledge with the lower.

(15) They are mighty and prompt to fulfil the will of the Deity, and their nature is endowed with such celerity that wherever the Divine glance bids then there they are straightway found. *(16) They are the guardians of the divisions of the earth; they are set over nations and regions, allotted to them by Their Creator; they govern all our affairs and bring us succor*. And the reason surely if because they are set over us by the divine will and command and *(17) are ever in the vicinity of God.*

---

[6] The translator and editor makes note of the underlying Greek of the text, which I reproduce here for its importance: εν νοητοις και τοποις.

[7] Here the editor and translator observes that the Damascene is alluding to the third chapter of St. Dionysius the Areopagite's *Celestial Hierarches*.

With difficulty are they moved to evil, yet they are not absolutely immoveable: but *(18) now they are altogether immoveable, not by nature but by grace and by their nearness to the Only Good.*

They behold God according to their capacity, and this is their food.

They are above us for they are incorporeal, and are free of all bodily passion, yet are not passionless: for the Deity alone is passionless.

(19) They take different forms at the bidding of their Master, God, and thus reveal themselves to men and unveil the divine mysteries to them.

They have Heaven for their dwelling-place, and have one duty, to sing God's praise and carry out His divine will.

Moreover, as that most holy, and sacred, and gifted theologian, Dionysius the Areopagite, says, All theology, that is to say, the holy Scripture, has nine different names for the heavenly essences. These essences that divine master in sacred things divides into three groups, each containing three. And the first group, he says, consists of those who are in God's presence and are said to be directly and immediately one with Him, viz., the Seraphim with their six wings, the many-eyed Cherubim and those that sit in the holiest thrones. The second group is that of the Dominions, and the Powers, and the Authorities; and the third, and last, is that of the Rulers[8] and Archangels and Angels.

Some, indeed, like Gregory the Theologian,[9] say that these were before the creation of other things. He thinks that the angelic and heavenly powers were first and that

---

[8] Rulers, i.e., Principalities (JPF, ed.)

[9] Saint Gregory of Nazianzus, one of the three Cappadocian Fathers of the fourth century, is commemorated as "the Theologian," by both the Eastern and Western Churches (where the term "the "Divine," in its archaic sense of a "theologian" is used in the calendar, as "St. Gregory the Divine.")

thought was their function. Others, again, hold that they were created after the first heaven was made. But all are agreed that it was before the formation of man. For myself, I am in harmony with the theologian. *(20) For it was fitting that the mental essence should be the first created, and then that which can be perceived, and finally man himself, in whose being both parts are united.*

But those who say that the angels are the creators of any kind of essence whatever are the mouth of their father, the devil. For since they are created things they are not creators. But He Who creates and provides for and maintains all things is God, who alone is uncreate and is praised and glorified in the Father, the Son, and the Holy Spirit.

CHAPTER IV

Concerning the devil and demons

(21) He who from among these angelic powers was set over the earthly realm, and into whose hands God committed the guardianship of the earth, was not made wicked in nature but was good, and made for good ends, and received from His Creator no trace whatever of evil in himself. But he did not sustain the brightness and the honour which the Creator had bestowed on him, and of his free choice was changed from what was in harmony to what was at variance with his nature, and became roused against God Who created him, and determined to rise in rebellion against Him; and he was the first to depart from good and become evil. For evil is nothing else than the absence of goodness, just as darkness also is absence of light. For goodness is the light of the mind, and, similarly, evil is the darkness of the mind. Light, therefore, being the work of the Creator and being made Good (for *God saw all that He made, and behold they were exceeding good*), produced darkness at his free-will. But along with him an innumerable host of angels subject to him were torn away

and followed him and shared in his fall. Wherefore, being of the same nature as the angels, they became wicked, turning away at their own free choice from good to evil.

Hence they have no power or strength against any one except what God in His dispensation hath conceded to them, as for instance, against Job and those swine that are mentioned in the Gospels. But when God has made the concession they do prevail, and are changed and transformed into any form whatever in which they wish to appear.

(22) Of the future both the angels of God and the demons are alike ignorant: yet they make predictions. God reveals the future to the angels and commends them to prophecy, and so what they say comes to pass. *But the demons also make predictions, sometimes because they see what is happening at a distance, and sometimes merely making guesses;* hence much that they say is false and they should not be believed, even though they do often in the way we have said, tell what is true. Besides they know the Scriptures.

All wickedness, then, and all impure passions are the work of their mind. But while the liberty to attack man has been granted to them, they have not the strength to overmaster any one: for we have it in our power to receive or not to receive the attack.[10]

This passage is as strange and breathtaking to me now as it was when I first read it over four decades ago in college, for if one did not know better, one might think it was written by some slightly tipsy quantum mechanics physicist trying to

[10] St. John of Damascus, *On the Orthodox Faith (De Fide Orthodoxa*), trans. from the Greek and ed., Rev. S.D.F. Salmond, D.D., F.E.I.S., *Nicene and Post-Nicene Fathers,* Vol. IX, *Hilary of Poitiers, John of Damascus* (Grand Rapids, Michigan: Wm. B. Eerdmans Publishing Company, 1997), pp. 18-20, emphases added.

explain the meaning and implications of the complicated equations on the blackboard to an audience of laymen. Indeed, one gains the impression that the Damascene is struggling to find adequate words for a phenomenon that lies outside the neat and tidy metaphysical categories of his day, just as quantum mechanics struggles to communicate through a language and culture formed largely by a physics unable to contain its contents and bursting through its tidy boundaries.

Consider only the odd set of assertions and their implications from the numbered and italicized portions of the passage just cited, and consider its "both-and" qualities, or, to use the quantum physicist's vocabulary, its "superposition" qualities. When one looks at this passage in this way, it becomes clear that the Damascene's description of angels and demons involves statements about the following five broad categories:

a) their *materiality and immateriality;*
b) their *"sempiternality,"* a term that will be explained in due course;
c) their *free-will* and *motion*;
d) their *position or place* and *ability to shape-shift;*
e) their *ability to communicate without words or sound.*

We will now consider each of these categories with reference to the specific language in the numbered parts of the passage.

a. The "Immaterial Materiality" of Angels

Points 1 and 2: From the outset of the passage, the Damascene confronts a typical misconception head-on. He begins by outlining angelic existence in fairly standard and familiar terms; they are "an incorporeal race" and a kind of "immaterial fire" and "a sort of spirit." They are "an intelligent essence" that is "in perpetual motion, with free-will." All this makes them bodiless, or "incorporeal." They are thus "borne to regions above" and are not given to material thoughts, presumably because they do not require food in the standard sense, and also because they are free of bodily passions.

Point 4: But just as soon as these standard and familiar points are expressed, he then qualifies them tremendously by the observation that everything created, including angels, when compared to "the Deity" which alone is "immaterial and incorporeal," is thus really "dense and material."

In other words, compared to man and animals and the rest of creation, angels are *much less "dense" and relatively immaterial*; but compared to the Deity, they too have some sort of "materiality." This implies that they are of such a super-fine matter that when compared to the rest of creation they are so "fine" that they are for all intents and purposes "immaterial." The Damascene is using a dialectic of oppositions between the material and corporeal on the one hand, and the immaterial and incorporeal on the other, to communicate a truth, namely, that angels cannot be comprehended in such simplistic binary terms; they exist in a continuum that lies somewhere between absolutely immateriality and absolute materiality.

(1) Their Ability to Penetrate Ordinary Matter and "Unlimited" Nature

Point 9: This "immaterial materiality" or "super-fine material condition" is the basis for yet another familiar concept, namely that they can move through solid objects because they cannot be contained within "walls and doors, bars or seals," and *this* because "they are quite unlimited." Or to put this differently, their "super-fine" and "immaterial

material" condition gives them a kind of unlimited extension. But this *too* is subjected to yet another strange qualification by the Damascene.

(2) Their Ability to Shapeshift

Points 10 and 19: This qualification of their "unlimited" but "fine material" condition is qualified by the statement that "it is not as they really are that they reveal themselves" to men, but "in a changed form which the beholders are capable of seeing." In more common modern terms, they are able, because of their bodiless but superfine material condition, to shapeshift, but only within prescribed boundaries determined by God (Point 19).

b. The Everlasting Temporality, or "Sempiternity," of Angels

Points 3, 6, 11, 19, and 22: Perhaps the strangest set of "angelic superposition" characteristics mentioned by the Damascene are those dealing with the relationship of angels and time. They possess an "immortal nature" which they have obtained "by grace," i.e., as a gift, from God. Yet, as creatures, they "begin to be," though their being—once brought into existence – does not end. Yet he goes on to say (in a manner similar to what he said in relationship to angelic materiality) that God alone is Eternal and the "creator of times" and therefore, "not under the dominion of time" but "above" it (Point 6). In other words, just as angels are material with respect to God but "immaterial" with respect to the rest of creation, so too with respect to God they exist in some sort of *temporal* state, but with respect to man and the rest of creation, they cannot die and are everlasting.

Additionally, the Damascene states "they have no *need* of marriage" because "they are immortal." (Point 11)[11]

This condition of a beginning and a continual state of existence, or immortality, confers on them a kind of everlasting temporality, a presence in all times *after* that in which they were created. In the Western Middle Ages the scholastics coined a term for this type of extreme temporal extension: "sempiternity." This condition doubtless forms a partial rationalization in the Damascene's mind for why angels do not need to reproduce. But there is another ability this sempiternity produces, and that is the ability to "make predictions" on account of being able to see "what *is happening* at a distance" (Point 22). *Note that the Damascene uses **the present tense** to describe this ability.* In other words, they do not make predictions about the future because they see the *future*, but rather, make predictions of the future (for us) because of what is already *present* to them by dint this strange temporal extension. Were one to put this condition in more modern terms, one might perhaps say that temporality for the angelic state is not merely a vector, because they are beings of vast spatial and temporal extension, and therefore, of vast memory, knowledge, and power.

c. Their Free Will and Motion

Points 5 and 18: This sempiternal condition is underscored by what he states concerning angelic free choice. Angels are, he notes, rational creatures endowed with free will, and as creatures they thus have the power "to abide *or progress in goodness* or to turn towards evil." (Point 5) Once again, however, the Damascene appears to produce another

---

[11] Note that the Damascene does not address the speculative question of whether or not angels *are able* to reproduce. He merely states that they have no *need* to do so.

contradiction when he later states (Point 18) that "*now* they are altogether immoveable, not by nature but by Grace and *by their nearness to the Only Good.*"

In other words, something about the *environment* conditions their will, the environment in this case being "their nearness" to God. Yet, earlier he has stated that they can progress in good, or turn to evil (and presumably, "progress" in that as well).

The mediaeval western scholastics resolved this dilemma in a very imaginative and creative fashion, one that actually did justice to what the Damascene was saying with his "superposition" language. Noting that angels are creatures and could have free choice, they could, of course, choose to rebel against God and to become, and to do, evil. And because that faculty of choice was a component of their nature, it never left them. *But additionally*, because they are "sempiternal" beings, that first exercise of choice immediately fixes their *habit* of will. They still have choices, but the choices are now environmentally conditioned by that habit, such that the choices are between various evils. Conversely, those that choose God and goodness also immediately fix the habit of their will, and all choices are good because the environment is conditioned by a good habit and intention.

A simple (and perhaps too simplistic) analogy might help to illustrate what is happening here. We in the West have been culturally conditioned to think that free choice must always be dialectically conditioned, that we must be able to choose evil to be truly free and have real free choice. But this is *not* the way the early Church tended to view it, and why the Eastern Churches to this day do not view it in the same way as the Western Churches.[12] Simply put, one may choose, for

[12] That so many in the west came to view it dialectically is intimately related to the recurring problem of free will and

example, to go grocery shopping today, or to get one's car tuned. Neither choice is "evil" and neither choice involved a moral dialectic. Similarly, one may choose to commit adultery or to gorge one's tastes for fine food and opulence. Both of these choices *are* entangled in a moral dialectic of evil," but notably, there is no moral dialectic of good and evil between them. Or finally, one may choose to grocery shop, or to gorge oneself on fine food and opulence or to commit adultery. In this case, there is a moral dialectic of opposition. We humans move *through* time as we move *through* space, and hence, our habit of will is formed over time and through several choices. Angels, by contrast, do not move through time or space as we do, and hence the habit of will is formed with the first choice. This does not mean no further choices are possible to them, but rather that those choices are environmentally conditioned by that habit: do I tune my car or grocery shop? Or do I commit adultery or gluttony? Thus the Damascene maintains in one and the same passage that angels have free choice, but yet that they are "immoveable" *in a particular moral condition*, and yet, nevertheless, can also *progress* in that condition via the exercise of choices. In short, there are three *kinds* of free choices: (1) those where all alternatives are good and not entangled with evil; (2) those where all alternatives are evil and devoid of good; and finally (3) those where there is a moral dialectic between a good choice, and an evil one.

---

predestination in the Western Churches, and that in turn is intimately related to the profound, and profoundly deleterious, influence of the theological formulations of St. Augustine of Hippo Regius on western Theology, from Papal to Presbyterian. This cultural-theological phenomenon is much too complex to delve into here. For an overview of it, see my *God, History, and Dialectic*, and particularly volume II, on Lulu.com.

d. The "Mental" Place, or Non-Local Position, of Angels; Both Circumscribed and Not

Points 8, 9, 12, 14, 16, 17, 21, 20, and 22: Once we have taken cognizance of the fact that free choice is best approached not simply from the point of view of the person or species exercising it, but also from the position of its moral habit and the environment of possible choices that are in turn not conditioned simply upon a moral dialectic, then we are also in a position to comprehend the Damascene's equally "super-positional" language about *the place, or location*, of Angels. If they are immaterial yet material, unlimited and incorporeal and yet material, then what of their spatial extension and location?

It is precisely here that the Damascene's language becomes even more focused in its "superpositional" character. For example, within two adjacent sentences, he uses language and concepts in one sentence that is directly and immediately contradicted by language in the following sentence:

> They are circumscribed, for when they are in the Heaven they are not on the earth, and when they are sent by God down to the earth, they do not remain in the Heaven. They are not hemmed in by walls and doors, and bars and seals, for they are quite unlimited. (Points 8 and 9)

Once again, we're dealing with superpositional language, in this case, not of an "immaterial materiality," but of an "unlimited circumscription." He goes on to clarify—or confuse—the issue by noting that since Angels are "intelligences" or "minds" that they are also "in mental places and are not circumscribed after the fashion of a body" nor are they "extended in three dimensions." (Point 12).

Note, however, that one may take away from this that they *are* in *some* sort of place or locality, but just not one limited to extension "in three dimensions." Then to confuse matters once again, they differ from each other "in brightness *and position*" (Point 14). Were the Damascene alive today, he perhaps would say that they possess a *hyper-dimensional* sort of extension and position, commensurate with their "unlimited circumscription" as sempiternal beings. He is describing beings that are quasi-ubiquitous, but which yet cannot be "present" everywhere, perhaps not as a matter of physical presence, but rather, as a matter of *intentional* presence. A simple analogy may once again aid in clarifying what he seems to be implying with this multiple-layered superpositional language.

Imagine you are standing in a doorway, with one foot planted in one room, and the other foot planted in an adjacent room. Which room are you in? *Physically and materially*, you are in both. But suppose now your conscious attention and mind are focused on what is transpiring in one room, even as your head and eyesight are diverted to the other. Which room are *you* in? By intention and focus, you are in one room while physically occupying or being present in both.

(1) Guardians of Regions and Boundaries

Indeed, the Damascene conjures just such an analogy by noting in Point 16 that angels "are the guardians of the divisions of the earth" because they are "set *over* nations and regions" thus governing "all our affairs." To put this differently, angels are guardians of the *boundary conditions* of of creation, and hence of political and ethnic borders and groups and actual regions. To put this point differently yet again, they are guardians of *topological regions or spaces*, and because of this, *of lower order regions and borders* such as political and ethnic divisions and regions. Yet, in spite of this "location" they are also, within a space of a few short sentences, said to be "*ever* in the vicinity of God." In other words, they now appear to be capable of a kind of "multi-location" or, to employ yet another physics metaphor, to be capable of a kind of non-locality, yet their willful focus or intention appears to "concentrate" that location.

(2) Man the Microcosm or Common Surface

Being guardians of the "divisions of the earth" angels are thus also guardians of the most crucial boundary condition or common surface of them all, man, for "it was fitting that the mental essence should be the first created, and then that which can be perceived, and finally man himself, in whose being both parts are united."(Point 20) That is to say, for St. John of Damascus, as for many Christian versions of the ancient doctrine of man-as-microcosm, man is a microcosm precisely because he has one foot firmly planted in both "rooms," the noetic, spiritual, "immaterial" room, and the material "room."

(3) The Position of Lucifer as Guardian of the Earth

Point 21: Then in Point 21 St. John points out that the angel appointed to the governorship of the earth *fell*, and became a demon. As will be seen in the next section, this is quite the crucial point, for in effect it means quite literally that the planet is *possessed, haunted*, and that it is a locus and focus of rebellion against God, the focus and battleground of an intense war. We shall have much more to say about this in due course, but for now, our attention must be directed to one of the most astonishing things of all in this passage…

(4) ...The "Angelic Uncertainty Principle."

The most concentrated and focused expression of the Damascene's superpositional language occurs in Point 13, which I call simply "The Angelic Uncertainty Principle," for with but a few changes of a few words, his statement could be recast as a classic statement of the Quantum Uncertainty Principle of Werner Heisenberg. Indeed, such language occurs almost nowhere else in any patristic or mediaeval literature, and one wonders exactly what was the inspiration and/or process of reasoning behind the statement. Regardless of what that inspiration and/or process of reasoning may have been, the statement itself is breathtaking both for its simplicity and implications:

> But to whatever post they may be assigned, there they are present after the manner of a mind and energise, ***and cannot be present <u>and</u> energise in various places at the same time.***

If one did not know this was a late seventh and early eighth century Church father, one might be forgiven for thinking that one was reading a slightly quirky version of the idea that one cannot measure the place of an electron and its momentum at the same time.

What the Damascene appears to be saying, however, seems clear enough, given everything else he has said about them. If angels are a kind of immaterial materiality, an unlimited circumscription, with beginning but without end, a quasi-ubiquitous extension in space and time and not limited or enclosed by three-dimensional material barriers, then they are capable of 'being present" in multiple dimensions or "mental places," but their energetic and wilful activity is constrained by the focus or intention of their will to *one* of those mental places, which mental places, let it be noted, *might appear to be in several places in normal "3D" space and its normal "3D" space observers.*

e. Their Ability to Communicate without Words or Sound: Entanglement

If this last example of "superpositional language" sounds all too inconveniently like the uncertainty principle of quantum mechanics, then their method of inter-communication sounds even more bizarrely "quantum mechanical." Why?

If they are "immaterial material" beings, of an unlimited circumscribed character, creatures in that they began to be, immortal in that they cannot end (and thus "sempiternal), located in "mental (high dimensional?) spaces, and of vast, quasi-ubiquitous extent, and thus "multi-locational" as being both with God yet "guardians of the divisions of the Earth," then how do they communicate?

Here the Damascene's language is, once again, oddly very close to quantum mechanics and its idea of "entanglement," for in Point 7 he states that "they have no need of tongue or hearing," and that "without uttering words they communicate to each other their own thoughts and counsels," thoughts and counsels, or information, or sets of information. This entanglement, let it be recalled, includes the future, which "they see *is* happening at a distance." "Words," in other words, are a very slow and inefficient way for sempiternal beings to communicate. The information to be communicated is entangled in their very being.

f. Summary of Conclusions

What all this seems to imply is that the Damascene views angels as

1) having a very fine "materiality";
2) having a kind of quasi-ubiquity, or vast extension, so vast, in fact, that they do not appear to material organisms to possess bodiliness, but are, rather, "bodiless";
3) having nevertheless a *kind* of extension in that they *are* in some sort of location;
4) which location is a mental, perhaps hyper-dimensional place;
5) given all of the above, they communicate without words, all of which implies a kind of entanglement; and finally, and most suggestively,
6) there is even a kind of "Angelic Uncertainty Principle" in the Damascene's formulations, so strongly suggestive of the modern quantum mechanical uncertainty principle, that I cannot view this resemblance as merely circumstantial.

With these thoughts in mind, we now turn to "the Epigraph," to Sitchen's incredible "demon in the *ekur*," the "demon in the pyramid," and *why* he's (actually, *she's*) there, and what *she's doing* there.

B. Sitchin and the Demon in the Ekur

All of these traditions and teachings about angels and demons bring us at last to the "epigraph" that I originally incorporated in the very first version of *The Giza Death Star* and which, when I re-wrote the book for submission to Adventures Unlimited Press, I omitted. This is the epigraph that I restored in *The Giza Death Star Revisited*, and which is the very *raison d'etre* for writing *this* book. The epigraph, as one might by now have come to expect, was a quotation from Zechariah Sitchin:

> An Akkadian "Book of Job" titled *Ludlul Bel Nimeqi* ("I praise the Lord of Deepness") refers to the "irresistible demon that has exited from the Ekur" in a land "across the horizon, in the Lower World (Africa)."[13]

As I pointed out in my previous book *The Cosmic War: Interplanetary Warfare, Modern Physics, and Ancient Texts*, the Akkadian term *ekur* can mean a "mountain," but it is also the same term used for a ziggurat or pyramid, the man-made mountains that one finds throughout Mesopotamia and, of course, "in the Lower World" that is "across the horizon," Egypt. As I also pointed out in that book, the word can also function at a further level of meaning, to indicate the "mountains" that emerge from the "sea" or "abyss" of space, i.e., the term can also mean, metaphorically, a planet.[14]

Now, here, in this quotation, all those meanings appeared concentrated in one expression, tied, moreover, to the presence of an "irresistible demon" who apparently at some point was located inside, perhaps even inhabiting, an "ekur," a "mountain" or pyramid. In this one quotation, all those themes—interplanetary warfare, mountains as both pyramids and planets, angels as guardians of planets and regions of

---

[13] Zechariah Sitchin, *The Wars of Gods and Men: The Third Book of the Earth Chronicles* (Santa Fe, New Mexico: Bear and Company, 1985, ISBN 093968090-4), p. 140.

[14] Q.v. Joseph P. Farrell, *The Cosmic War: Interplanetary Warfare, Modern Physics, and Ancient Texts: A Study in Non-Catastrophist Interpretations of Ancient Legends* (Kempton, Illinois: Adventures Unlimited Press, 2007, ISBN978-1-931882-75-0), pp. 75-79, 82-83, 294 for a discussion of the mountains⁀planets⁀pyramids⁀weapons formula of the various meanings associated with the Akkadian term *ekur*.

planets, and Lucifer as the fallen and demonic guardian of Earth, and of course Sitchin's idea of the Great Pyramid as some sort of weapon involved in those wars—came together in one very concentrated and inconvenient sentence.

Why inconvenient?

Because difficult as it is to advance very putative and speculative physics and arguments able to explain or rationalize that structure as a very powerful weapon, throwing a demon into that mix only increases the stakes and the difficulty, for how does one explain its presence? On one level, it is very easy to rationalize, for the presence of something so personally evil, and powerful, would explain why such weapons were built and used. In other words, it is very easy to suggest that this is simply a bit of poetic metaphor, a rationalization and personification of the evil use of a technology.

But what if the demon's presence in the *ekur* or pyramid was something *more*? What if the quotation means not something metaphorical, but a very *real* demon occupying a very *real* pyramid? Moreover, what if, in some fashion, its presence actually formed a component of the weapon system itself? If that's the case, in what way does this modify the weapon hypothesis? How might a demonic presence actually "work" in such an instance?

When I first read this quotation, in other words, I immediately realized its importance to the weapon hypothesis, and yet also its extreme difficulty of being incorporated into it. This book is consequently an attempt to give speculative answers to these questions. It is quite important to understand that the weapon hypothesis does *not* stand or fall on the basis of what follows.

Nevertheless, once one acknowledges the strange characteristics of angels such as outlined by St. John of Damascus or other writers on the subject, then the relevance of those properties to the weapon hypothesis is impossible to dismiss. All these angelic characteristics—a kind of quasi-ubiquity (or if one prefer the modern term, non-locality), a vast extension in space and time, the ability to see the future (and presumably the past up to a point) as if it is the present with the commensurate implied abilities of pre- and retro-causation, the ability to "communicate" by what appears to be a kind of entanglement, and above all the very fact that one is dealing with a "bodiless" and purely "intellectual" life-form, that is to say, *with a non-organic life form* of vast spatial and temporal extent, with the *memory and knowledge and intelligence* that extension all implies—all these things cannot help but profoundly modify the weapon hypothesis by their mere presence in the equation. For those of a New Agey "jonquils and daisies" approach who whistle endlessly about occult influences and higher consciousness and so on, all the while decrying merely physical approaches, well, here it is, in spades.

The rest of this book is focused on these questions and issues, but first we must deal once again with the issue of Sitchin's translation of the text, in this case the text of the *Ludlul Bel Nimeqi.*

1. Sitchin's Translation vis-a-vis His Approach to Mesopotamian Texts

But why should the *Ludlul Bel Nimeqi* even be referring to the Great Pyramid at all? It is, after all, a *Mesopotamian* text, and Egypt is hundreds of miles from Mesopotamia, and for that matter, the wedges of cuneiform ideograms bear little to no resemblance to the carefully executed artistry of Egyptian hieroglyphics.

Sitchin himself was aware of this problem, and commented extensively upon it, and his comments moreover form the context in which our "demon-in-the-pyramid" quotation occurs:

> We have found many similarities between these unique features of the Great Pyramid and the pre-Diluvial E.KUR ("House Which is Like a Mountain") of Enlil, his ziggurat in Nippur. Like the Great Pyramid, it rose high to dominate the surrounding plain. In pre-Diluvial times the Ekur of Nippur housed the DUR.AN.KI—"Link Heaven-Earth"—and served as Mission Control Center, equipped with the Tablets of Destinies, the orbital data panels. It also contained the DIR.GA, a mysterious "Dark Chamber" whose "radiance" guided the shuttlecraft to a landing at Sippar.
>
> But all that—the many mysteries and functions of the Ekur described in the tale of Zu—was before the Deluge. When Mesopotamia was reinhabited and Nippur was reestablished, the abode of Enlil and Ninlil there was a large temple surrounded by courtyards, with gates through which the worshipers could enter. It was no longer forbidden territory; the space-related functions, as the Spaceport itself, had shifted elsewhere.
>
> As a new, mysterious, and awesome Ekur, the Sumerian texts described a "House Which is Like a Mountain" in a distant place, under the aegis of Ninhursag, not of Enlil. Thus, the epic tale of an early post-Diluvial Sumerian king named Etana, who was taken aloft toward the Celestial Abode of the Annunaki, states that his ascent began not far from the new Ekur, at the "Place of the Eagles"—not far, that is, from the Spaceport. An Akkadian "Book of Job" titled *Ludlul Bel Nimeqi* ("I praise the Lord of Deepenss") refers to the "irresistible demon that has exited from the Ekur" in a land "across the horizon in the Lower World (Africa)"
>
> Not recognizing the immense antiquity of the Giza pyramids or the identity of their true builders, scholars have also been puzzled by this apparent reference to an Ekur far

> from Sumer. Indeed, if one is to follow accepted interpretations of Mesopotamian texts, no one in Mesopotamia was ever aware of the existence of the Egyptian pyramids. None of the Mesopotamian kings who invaded Egypt, none of the merchants who traded with her, none of the emissaries who had visited there—not one of them had noticed these colossal monuments.
>
> Could that be possible?
>
> We suggest that the Giza monuments *were* known in Sumer and Akkad. We suggest that the Great Pyramid was the post-Diluvial Ekur, of which the Mesopotamian texts did speak at length (as we shall soon show). *And we suggest that ancient Mesopotamian drawings depicted the pyramids during their construction and after they had been completed!*
>
> *We have already shown what the Mesopotamian "pyramids"—the ziggurats or stage-towers—looked like. We find completely* ***different*** *structures on some of the most archaic Sumerian depictions. In some we see the construction of a structure with a square base and triangular sides—a smooth-sided pyramid. Other depictions show a completed pyramid.*
>
> …
>
> And yet another endows the completed pyramid with wings, to indicate its space-related function….
>
> … Indeed, even in such a minor detail as the precise slope of the Great Pyramid—52°—the Sumerian depiction appears to be accurate.[15]

In other words, it is the *pictures* that compel Sitchin to interpret the texts in reference to the Great Pyramid and the

---

[15] Zechariah Sitchin, *The Wars of Gods and Men*, pp. 140-142, emphasis added.

Giza complex, and to Egypt in general, and not just the texts alone. These pictures, as he pointed out, depict pyramids that look nothing like the stepped pyramids or ziggurats of Mesopotamia. This very real world correspondence between ancient Sumerian pictures are what lead Sitchin to translate words such as "lower world" not in terms of some sort of primeval "abyss," but much more literally as a metaphorical reference to Africa, or words such as "horizon" to indicate regions beyond Mesopotamia.

To buttress his argument, he reproduces the following pictures of the old Sumerian drawings:

Early Sumerian Depictions of a Smooth-Sided Pyramid[16]

The Early Sumerian Depiction of a Smooth-Sided Pyramid with wings[17]

---

[16] Zechariah Sitchin, *The Wars of Gods and Men*, p. 141.
[17] Zechariah Sitchin, *The Wars of Gods and Men*, p. 142.

Sitchin's interpretation of this last picture of the smooth-sided pyramid with wings as indicating a rocket spaceport that forms such a central component of his overall macro-scenario is suggestive. But once one recognizes, with Sitchin, its symbolic nature, then it might just as easily function as a symbol for *other* "space-related" ideas, including the idea that the pyramids have something to do with the nature of space *itself*, rather than having to do with space *travel*. Moreover, within the context of the "demon-in-the-pyramid" quotation, the wings which have since become part of the iconographic depictions of angels and demons might just as easily form a symbol of the demonic presence of his own text as well, thus tying together the idea of demons to pyramids once again.

There is, in fact, a very suggestive picture reproduced by Sitchin that more exactly symbolizes this demon-pyramid relationship:

Early Sumerian Picture of A Smooth-Sided Pyramid with Cadduceus-Ouroboros[18]

Observe that this picture combines a very complex association of symbolisms. Most notable is the clear depiction of entwined serpents in a kind of "horizontal caduceus," an

[18] Zechariah Sitchin, *The Wars of Gods and Men*, p. 141,

ancient symbol of wisdom, alchemy, and medical science. Of course, a serpent is also a symbol of the demonic and infernal. But notice just how *complex* this apparently simple and crude picture really is.

For example: the two snakes of the "horizontal caduceus" are entwined in *opposite directions,* with the snake on top moving to the right, and almost appearing to swallow its tail like yet another ancient symbol, that of the ouroboros, the snake-in-a-circle, swallowing its tail. The snake on the bottom moves in the *opposite* direction, and appears to be almost swallowing *its* tail. We thus have two intertwined (and ortho- or counter-rotating!) caduceuses as ouroboroi.

Now note *where* the two ortho-rotated or counter-rotating ouroboroi-cum-caduceuses appear to *meet*: *directly over the smooth-sided pyramid,* almost as if, in the symbolism itself, we are being warned that the structure has a demonic ability to manipulate temporal effects *in either direction, past, or future!*

2. Other Translations

So what about the texts themselves, and the text of the L*udlul Bel Nimeqi* in particular? Is Sitchin's argument that some Sumerian texts should and must be interpreted in reference to actual places and objects in Egypt correct? Is his translation of the demon-in-the-pyramid passage of the *Ludlul Bel Nemeqi* correct, or at least, *reasonable*? Here the answer would appear to be, if not a resounding shouted "yes!" then at least a *firm* one. There is a 2019 translation of the text—which itself is a beautiful and almost psalm-like meditation on the sufferings of the righteous—by Alan Lenzi and sponsored by the University of the Pacific.[19]

Here the demon-in-the-pyramid passage is translated as follows:

> Debilitating sickness advanced against me,
> Evil wind (from) the (hor)izon blew against me.
> Headache cropped up from the surface of the netherworld,
> A wicked demon/cough came forth from its Apsu.
> An un(relen)ting ghost came forth from Ekur,
> Lamashtu c(am)e down from the midst of the mountain.[20]

Here Sitchin's "irresistible demon" has become an "unrelenting ghost," who nonetheless as a demon (or cough) "came forth from its Apsu." This is suggestive, because Apsu can mean a kind of primordial abyss or netherworld. In any case, the text as translated by Lenzi is not far from Sitchin, for in both cases an "irresistible demon" or "unrelenting ghost" has come out of the ekur or "midst of the mountain."

The "evil wind from the horizon" is an intriguing reference, for elsewhere in *The Wars of Gods and Men* Sitchin has interpreted this "evil wind" as radioactive fallout born on the wind over Mesopotamia after one of his wars of gods and men involved the use of nuclear weapons. If Sitchin is to be faulted, it is simply for viewing "Apsu" and "horizon" as words having real geographical references to a land somewhere over the "horizon" and a "netherworld" or "Apsu," a "land below" which he understands to be Africa. But notably, Sitchin has not *translated* these terms as such, but rather, provided an editorial note about how he has

---

[19] *Ludlul Bel Nemeqi*, trans. Alan Lenzi, scholarlycommons.pacific.edu/cgi/viewcontant.cgi?article-1189&context=cop-facbooks

[20] Ibid., p. 5.

interpreted "netherworlds" or "lower world" as "Africa," and hence how he has interpreted the text not as metaphor or poetry, but as preserving the kernel of a memory of a real event. There is nothing, in other words, in Lenzi's translation that is at dramatic variance with Sitchin's translation, and indeed, one may interpret this particular passage as translated by Lenzi in a manner consistent with Sitchin's. Again, it is not the text alone which compels Sitchin to a "literal" interpretation; it is rather the text taken in conjunction with those ancient Sumerian depictions of smooth-sided, "Egyptian"-style pyramids.

If we turn to yet another translation of the same passage, that of Benjamin R. Foster, we encounter the same association of evil winds, and of demons (in this case, a female demon) with a "mountain":

> An evil vapor has blown against me
> (from the) ends of the earth.
> Head pain has surged up upon me from the breast of hell,
> A malignant spectre has come forth from its hidden depth,
> A relentless gho(st) cane out of its dwelling place.
> A she-demon came down from the mountain,
> Ague set forth with the flood.[21]

Clearly there are differences between these translations, but the overall effect remains the same in its central and core conception: a demon is associated with a mountain, or ekur, or pyramid.

---

[21] Benjamin R. Foster, ed. and trans., *Before the Muses: An Anthology of Akkadian Literature* (Bethesda, Maryland: CDL Press, 2005 ISBN 1883053-765), p. 400. This is a very thorough and extensive collection of Akkadian literature, ritual, poetry, and prayers, and the beauty of these works alone is well worth the price of the book.

In this respect it is interesting to note that Foster's translation later speaks of the conflict between Markduk and the "she-demon" in words that recall Lenzi's translation, and which again repeat the association of the "she-demon" with a "mountain":

> (He [Marduk] sent) down the malignant spectre to its hidden depth,
> The relentless ghost he returned (to) its dwelling,
> He overthrew the she-demon, sending it off to a mountain...[22]

There are three things to note regarding this brief comparison between Sitchin's and these more standard "academic" translations of the same passage:

1) Firstly, in no version of the passage is the association of the demon-in-the-pyramid/ekur/mountain broken or rendered obscure or unclear. On the contrary, the central conceptual core of Sitchin's version is preserved;
2) Secondly, it is also clear that Sitchin interprets the passage as referring to a real event that took place in identifiable locations, and even though the other two translations do not do so, they may nonetheless be interpreated with "Sitchinesque" eyes; and finally,
3) The other translators of this passage make *no reference to the artistic depiction of smooth-sided pyramids, their non-resemblance to any Mesopotamian pyramidal architectures, and their clear resemblance to those in the land of Egypt*. In short, Sitchin has furnished clear and unmistakable *reasons* for his interpretive paradigm. No other translator of the

[22] Ibid., p. 404.

> passage has done so, and this strongly implies that Sitchin also understood the significance of the association of demons with pyramids in the context of his *Wars of Gods and Men* scenario.

What he may not have seen or perhaps only intuited was the significance of this association for a much narrower idea of his: the weapon hypothesis of the Great Pyramid, one of the weapons of the Gods that made that war possible.

3. An Only Slightly Unnecessary and Tangential Excursion: Two Speculations about the Inscription on the Actual Entrance of the Great Pyramid:
a. The Khufu Cartouche and Cultural Expropriation of the Site and Building

There is one aspect of the physical structure of the Great Pyramid that I have not previously discussed in any of my books about it. In fact, it is a feature that is *seldom* discussed in all the vast literature that has been published about it, because no one knows exactly what it means or symbolizes, or indeed, if it is meant to mean or symbolize anything of significance at all. When Caliph Al-Maimun blasted his way into the pyramid in the ninth century in search of treasure, it is thought that perhaps one reason he might have done so was that some of the casing stones were still on the structure, covering the actual entrance, located some way up on the building on its north face. When the actual entrance *was* finally discovered, it proved to be a massive corbeled structure, and it also proved to be the only place with an inscription chiseled into the stone. The only book I have ever been able to find that has mentioned, depicted, and discussed this strange structure and inscription is André Pochan's *L'Énigme de la Grande Pyramide*, published in 1971 in

France.[23] M. Pochan's diagram depicts the location on the upper right corbel stone that was placed there during the Prussian expedition early in the 19th century.

But beneath the double corbelled stones, on a smaller stone with a boss exactly in the center of the stone, there are four enigmatic carved figures, figures that look *nothing* like any form of Egyptian hieroglyphic (with perhaps a couple of exceptions), and that look nothing like any cuneiform either:

Pochan's Diagram of the Entrance Inscription[24]

This inscription, as can be seen, M. Pochan calls the "enigmatic sculpted tetragrammaton" on the entrance.

M. Pochan provides the following diagram of the entrance, and depiction of the inscription, with the small letter "M" denoting where the inscription is located:

---

[23] André Pochan, *L'Énigme de la Grande Pyramide* (Paris: Éditions Robert Laffont, 1971), pp. 24-26. For yet another one of those "odd coincidences," it is worth noting, for those paying *really* close attention, that Editions Robert Laffont lists 6, place Saint-Sulpice, Paris-6a as the actual business address of the firm.

[24] Ibid., p. 25.

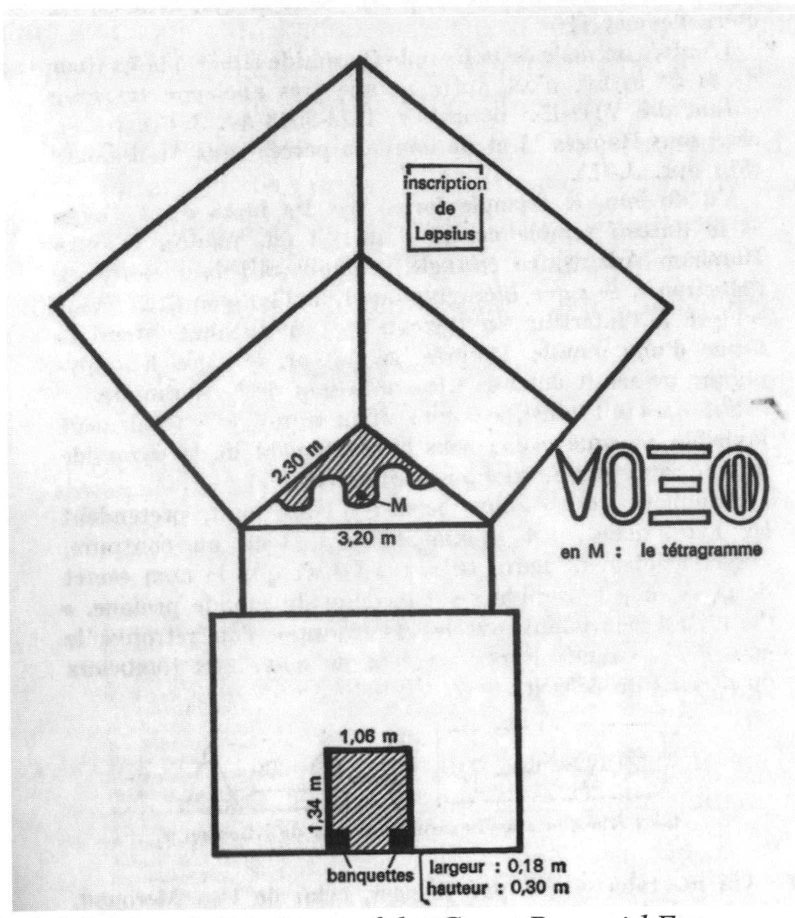

André Pochan's Diagram of the Great Pyramid Entrance and the location of the mysterious sculpted "tetragrammation"[25]

b. A (Terrible?)Tetragrammaton?

Note that Pochan also indicates the location of the 19th century Prussian expedition inscription that was put on the entrance by its leader, Lepsius, an inscription which ridiculously (?) states the Prussian King, Friedrich-Wilhelm IV is the Son of Ra![26] This later German graffiti covers a

[25] André Pochan, *L'Énigme de la Grande Pyramide,* p. 25.
[26] André Pochan, *L'Énigme de la Grande Pyramide,* p. 26.

much larger area than the "tetragrammaton" inscription, which looks curiously un-Egyptian, with perhaps only the last two glyphs—the three horizontal lines, and the three vertical lines inside the circle—being the only things that are possibly Egyptian, since they resemble hieroglyphic spellings of Khufu. Given the increasing doubts associated with Colonel Vyse's "discovery" of hieroglyphs in the so-called relieving chambers above the King's Chamber—a "discovery" that I believe to be a complete hoax perpetrated by Vyse himself as I outlined in *The Giza Death Star Revisited*—this "tetragrammaton" may be the only inscription on the Great Pyramid that attributes or connects the structure to the pharaoh Khufu. Pochan suggests that the name of the Great Pyramid, its "divine name," is "the luminous horizon of Khufu," because of the resemblance of the boss on the entrance represented by the shaded area:

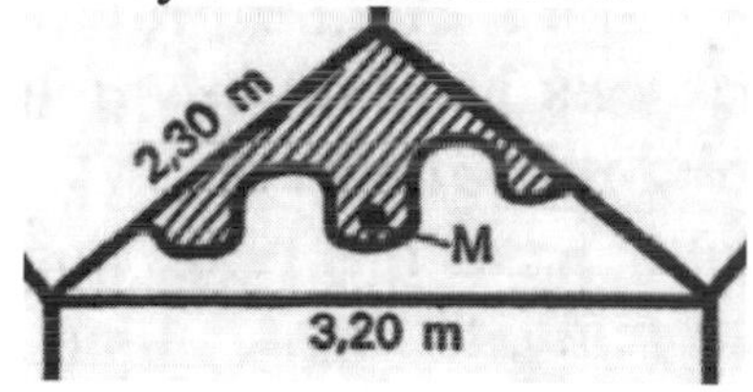

Close up of the Boss on the entrance, with "M" denoting the position of the "tetragrammaton" inscription

to the Egyptian hieroglyph for "horizon":

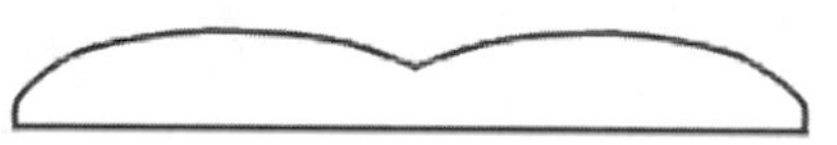

Eyptian Hieroglyph for "Horizon"

Notice that the hieroglyph in this case has two mounds, as if symbolically depicting the two large pyramids at Giza. In any case, Pochan's idea that the last two glyphs, which strongly resemble one of the signs for Khufu, occurring as they do in a boss on the entrance which in turn strongly resembles the hieroglyph for "horizon," might be a clue to the decryption of the enigmatic "tetragrammaton" inscription.

It *is* an ingenious explanation and in many respects a satisfactory one.

There is, however, one glaring problem, and that is that the last two signs on the "tetragrammaton" only *resemble* some of the various Egyptian glyphs for Khufu. The problem with the three horizontal lines is that they do not occur in a cartouche oval, and the three vertical ones, which *do* occur in an oval, are not—as far as the current state of knowledge—a glyph for Khufu.

The *other* problem is that we really have no good way of knowing *when* these signs were actually carved. Were they carved by the pyramid's builders, or much later by someone else who, like Lepsius, is adding a bit of graffiti to the site? I tend to accept the view that it was inscribed by the original builders, with the proviso that these builders were not Egyptian but some much older group, and that the tetragrammaton inscription probably means something, and indeed, may even be the name of the "demon in the ekur," or it may be the name of the ekur, or both. Ingenious as Pochan's explanation is, I suspect it simply is not adequate for the above reasons. We will probably never know.

4. "Plasma Cosmotheology"
a. Ekurs, Pyramids, and Demons: Mexico

Whether or not the "tetragrammaton" on the entrance of the Great Pyramid has anything to do with Sitchin's "demon in the *ekur*," one should remember that an ocean and a continent and half a world away from Giza, there is another culture, far removed both spatially and temporally from Egypt and Mesopotamia, whose texts *also* connect "demons" with "pyramids," and with the grizzly practice of human sacrifice tied with both. In my book *The Grid of the Gods: The Aftermath of the Cosmic War and the Physics of the Pyramid Peoples*, I pointed out that the Aztec creation myth, as recorded in the *Codex Chimalpopoca*, clearly states that human sacrifice was *prohibited* by their creator God, Quetzlcoatl, but later introduced by three demons who sound oddly like the three murderers of Hiram Abiff in Masonic lore of the master mason ritual, Jubelo, Jubela, Jubelum.[27]

The importance of the association of pyramids and demons for the Mexica peoples, and for Sitchin's observation that a "demon" was associated with the Great Pyramid, has to be pondered carefully, for in a general way the Mexican version tends to corroborate the view that the association itself forms some traumatic part of human memory. But there's something else it implies. In the case of Sitchin's quotation, one is dealing with texts that are older than the Aztec *Codex Chimalpopoca,* and the association of a demon with a pyramid is itself very *specific*: it occurs in the context of a war (and hence, great loss of life), and a specific *pyramid*, the Great Pyramid and the Giza complex in particular. By the time the association arrives in Mexico, one is dealing with demons in general and pyramids in general, still associated with great loss of life in the form of human sacrifice, which in turn is viewed as a kind of tributary payment to "the gods" to ward off their wrath. I am therefore suggesting that what began as a specific though most likely garbled memory, ended as an even more garbled memory,

---

[27] Joseph P. Farrell, with Scott D. deHart, *The Grid of the Gods: The Aftermath of the Cosmic War and the Physics of the Pyramid Peoples* (Kempton, Illinois: Adventures Unlimited Press, 2011 ISBN978-935487-39-5), pp. 204-211.

while nevertheless preserving the essential core of that memory, namely, the association of demons and demonic power with pyramidal structures.

b. Richard Hoagland:
Stars, Egyptian Religion, and Dante Alighieri

So what can possibly unite all these disparate and seemingly disconnected ideas? What common thread weaves together the Aeropagite's and the Damascene's angels and demons, with their "immaterial materiality" and their "sempiternity," their "unlimited" nature and their vast extension in time and space, and yet their inability to be in more than one place at the same time? What thread stiches together demons and pyramids, and *why*?

Years ago, pondering yet another aspect of this vast and intricate puzzle, author and Mars anomaly researcher Richard C. Hoagland asked a similar question in a very different context at his well-known lecture and presentation on the Mars anomalies at the United Nations:

> Science is nothing if it is not prediction. The discovery of specific signatures now on planets as diverse as Mars and Saturn, corresponding to predictions made by the Monuments of Mars, opens up literally overwhelming possibilities, not just for pushing clouds around on planets or positioning volcanoes, but for something dealing with the sources of the energy to *do* these things.
>
> Let me give you a couple of interesting examples.
>
> The Voyager missions a couple of years ago flew by the last planet of the system, Neptune. They measured during the fly-by the fact that inexplicably Neptune is emitting almost three times more energy than it's getting from the Sun. Question: Where is the energy coming from? No one currently knows. It is our profound suspicion that the

physics we have decoded at Cydonia is telling us about a hyper-dimensional source for this new energy.

Or take the Sun itself.

For the last several years scientists have been looking for particles that are supposed to be coming from the center of the Sun because of its thermonuclear reaction, a kind of "chained H-bomb" model. Well, for the last twenty years they haven't found anywhere *near* as many of these particles as models would predict. In fact, the Soviets and Japanese have recently brought on line experiments that measured fundamental particles and found none. Is it possible that the very center of our solar system—this incredible blazing ball of gas around which all the worlds in this system orbit—is in fact fueled from another source? The fact for instance that its sunspots peak at the key 19.5 latitude may be the clue.

Well, this opens up remarkable possibilities which, when you look back on cultures on this planet and their attention to the Sun, others may also have noticed.

...

When we look, then, at the stars, at the sky at night, we're not seeing chained and imprisoned H-bombs, we're seeing portals to another dimension. And the portals are glowing windows through which we can peer and glimpse the fragment of a physics from another side. What is stunning is when you take that metaphor and you go back and read the actual Egyptian descriptions and the hieroglyphics for Sirius, the brightest star in the sky, the description is, Sirius is a doorway.

Now, what did they know? What did they know?[28]

---

[28] Richard C. Hoagland, *Hoagland's Mars* (New Science Ideas, 4 DVD set, DVD #2, *The United Nations Breifing*), from time stamps 36:07-38:53.

Indeed, the ancient Egyptians were obsessed and possessed by a very peculiar religion, with immortality and with becoming stars, which were one and the same thing to them.

They were obsessed, in other words, with an afterlife wherein humans would be literally transformed into hot glowing balls of *plasma*. It's a decidedly strange idea, one as strange as Dante Alighieri's vision of the devil, being forever frozen at the center of hell, beating his wings furiously to escape, thereby only dissipating more heat, and enchaining him in more frozen hell, at the center of a cone of nine rings of decreasing diameter, rather like an inverted pyramid. The image of demons and pyramids, it seems, will not go away.

The Egyptian image of becoming immortal stars oddly recalls the Damascene's description of angels as a "kind of immaterial fire." Had he known the word, and how it fulfilled almost all of his strange descriptions of angels—as immaterially material, as both "unlimited" and yet "circumscribed," of vast spatial and temporal extent, power, and memory, of a "less dense" state of materiality than the rest of creation, as able to penetrate or go through solid walls and doors, and as something able to describe both the vast and cold and nearly empty interstices of space, or the blazing hot balls of gas we call stars—he would have used the term "plasma." But he would have been entirely correct in maintaining that these were living, intelligent, beings, a kind of "inorganic life," because on *that* view the only thing lacking in his description is the term plasma itself. All the other conceptions—perhaps to the chagrin of scientism—are there. So, are some plasmas possibly alive and intelligent? To that question, we now turn.

3
Aether Plasmaniferous: The Plasma-Life Hypothesis

"Ye are of your father the devil, and the lusts of your father ye will do: he was a murderer from the beginning, and abode not in the truth, because there is no truth in him. When he speaketh a lie, he speaketh of his own: for he is a liar, and the father of it."

"Verily, verily, I say unto you, Before Abraham was, I am."
Christ, Gospel of St. John, 8:44, 58.

If Angels—and therefore demons—are a form of inorganic plasma-based life, then the relevance of that idea to the Weapon Hypothesis of the Great Pyramid becomes immediately apparent, for if, as Christopher Dunn speculated, hydrogen gas was found inside the Great Pyramid,[1] and if, as I speculated, it may have existed in an endothermic plasma state in a plasma pinch,[2] then the structure becomes not just a machine, but minimally a habitation and possibly even a prosthetic and a kind of electro-acoustic-bio-weapon. One is even tempted to advance the extremely speculative hypothesis that the dimensional analogues in the structure are designed to be coupled harmonic oscillators not only of the planet and local space, but of their angelic guardian, a guardian whom, as we saw, the Damascene understood to be a fallen angel or demon. Similarly, one is tempted to advance the idea that pyramids-as-demonic dwellings and oscillators, as types of prosthetic

[1] Christopher Dunn, *The Giza Powerplant* (Santa Fe, New Mexico: Bear and Company, 1998 ISBN 978-1-879181-50-9), pp. 182-200.

[2] Joseph P. Farrell, *The Giza Death Star* (Corviss Press Reprint, Lulu, 2023), pp. 197ff.

bio-weapons designed for, and activated by, certain "plasma-spirits" in their capacity as governors of specific nations and regions, might rationalize the presence not only of pyramids over the surface of the planet, but also the grizzly and bloody activity associated with so many of them.

All of that is, however, extreme speculation, one which is moreover dependent upon the underlying notion that plasmas might indeed be the kind of "bodiless" and inorganic, "immaterial- material" life implied by traditional teachings on angels and demons. There are two components to that case, the case which we now examine and advance in this and the next chapter:

1) That there are specific reasons arguing for the view that some plasmas constitute a form of (inorganic) life; and,
2) That there are specific reasons arguing for the view that some plasmas constitute a form of (inorganic) *intelligent and self-aware* life.

The hypothesis of plasma life must be phrased in this specific way to avoid the pitfall of the implication that all plasmas *are* a form of life, or a form of intelligent life. We are advancing the notion only that *some* plasmas may be alive, and of these, only that *some* may be self-aware and intelligent.

It is also crucial to understand one more point about the methodology that I am following here. I am *not* arguing for the case that angels and demons are plasmas or conversely that plasmas are the kind of self-aware intelligences represented by angels and demons. I am, rather, *accepting* that case as "true for the sake of argument," and noting the general implications of that hypothesis for how easily and neatly it fulfills most traditional teachings regarding such creatures, and noting the particular implications of that hypothesis for the Weapon Hypothesis of the Great Pyramid.

It is also crucial to understand that these implications are (and were) entailed in Sitchin's quotation regarding the "demon in the *ekur*" at the outset, and that I omitted this quotation in the revised version of *The Giza Death Star* that was eventually published. My reason for the omission was that, twenty years ago, the argument that some plasma might be alive and even intelligent was just beginning to be made. Indeed, the famous quantum and plasma physicist David Bohm had tentatively advanced the idea of plasmas as life forms, but twenty years ago, and even more so in *his* day, there was no body of literature on the subject. Additionally, the core argument of the Weapon Hypothesis did not and does not require it. Now, however, there *is* a body of literature on the subject which can be reviewed, and its implications for the Weapon Hypothesis can be explored.

No one has argued the case for plasma life forms more completely and thoroughly than has British scientist, archaeologist, and thinker Robert Temple, in an exciting book published in 2021 titled *A New Science of Heaven*. Temple's book is, in fact, the best compendium of all the thought about the plasma-life hypothesis under one cover thus far published and easily available to the public, and we shall thus follow his presentation closely throughout the remainder of this book.

However, though Robert Temple is the first to attempt to gather all the speculation about the plasma life hypothesis in one book, the hypothesis itself has its origins in two notions, the general plasma "cosmology" of Swedish Nobel Laureate in Physics, Hannes Alfvén, and a particular observation of the quantum and plasma physicist David.

A. Plasma Physicist David Bohm's Observation, and the Beginning of the Plasma Life Hypothesis

On numerous occasions and in various contexts during the years intervening between the publication of the original *Giza Death Star* trilogy and the "update" in *The Giza Death Star Revisited*, I often remarked or commented about the strange observation of David Bohm regarding plasmas as life forms. During that time I was often asked where one might find out more about it, and the difficulty, as I remarked on those occasions, was that "everyone" in physics seemed to know about it, but it seemed as if few wanted to talk about it. One gained the impression that some were even embarrassed by it. After all, David Bohm was one of physics' premier names and thinkers, and his textbook on quantum mechanics is still regarded as a classic in the field. The textbook is, so to speak, a part of the physics literature "canon."

A young David Bohm (1917-1992), possibly around the time of his involvement with the Manhattan Project

Professor Bohm

David Bohm in later life

So when someone of his stature voices the idea that plasmas might be alive, one tends either to brush off the idea as a rare eccentric "slip of the tongue" by one of the world's otherwise more brilliant physics minds ("there goes David again, off on another one of his plasma fantasies"), or one can delve more deeply. The trouble is, until a biography was finally published about Bohm in 1996, no one in the broader public beyond the plasma physics community really knew what Bohm had actually discovered nor what he really thought about it.

In this respect, a brief overview of Bohm's life might be helpful to illustrate two possible influences upon him that led him eventually to formulate such a radical hypothesis and view.

David Joseph Bohm was born on December 20, 1917 to a Hungarian-Jewish-American family in Wilkes-Barre, Pennsylvania. The name "Bohm" was an Anglicization of the family's Hungarian surname Düm. His parents' marriage was not a happy one, but Bohm and his younger brother grew up in a fairly comfortable middle class American life that their father's furniture business provided. While Bohm later became agnostic, he and his father—with whom he did not otherwise get along—were friendly with a cultured and widely read rabbi, and in this long family tradition of Judaism with its seraphim and cherubim and other angelic beings, Bohm probably imbibed an ability to view life itself as involving more than just "organic compounds."

The second influence upon Bohm was his predilection to relieve the stresses of homelife and the tensions between his mother—for whom he had a deep love and affection—and his querulous father by reading popular science fiction pulp magazines and stories. Bohm thus gave free rein to his imagination via science fiction, always insisting, however, that his (or anyone else's!) science fiction be grounded in and mindful of actual real science and not mere wishful thinking.[3]

---

[3] F. David Peat, *Infinite Potential: The Life and Times of David Bohm* (Perseus Publishing: 1997 ISBN 978-0201328202), pp. 5-9. Peat's biography is not a standard biography, for he was a friend of

So what exactly did Bohm discover?

According to his long-time friend and biographer F. David Peat, Bohm, like many scientists in the early 1940's who were being considered to work on the USA's atom bomb project, fell under suspicion for his left-wing and—in Bohm's case—clearly Marxist and Communist views. While many scientists including Robert Oppenheimer himself were eventually cleared to work on the project, Bohm had to wait until 1943 when a British physicist, H.S.W. Massey, took over the Radiation Laboratory to conduct tests on uranium plasmas. While not directly a part of the Manhattan Project, these experiments were definitely connected to Manhattan Project research, and thus Bohm, in spite of his Marxist and Communist beliefs, became an unwitting participant in the project, creating a uranium plasma for use in cyclotrons.[4]

It was while working on this project that Bohm made his observation about plasmas, which in turn led to "his first outstanding contribution to physics."[5]

> In order to accelerate and direct the uranium atoms in the cyclotron beams, it was first necessary to strip them of some of their outer electrons and leave them with a positive charge. The resulting collection of free electrons and positively charged atoms is known generically as a plasma, *a fourth state of matter quite distinct from a solid, liquid, or gas.* In a plasma, positively charged nuclei and negatively charged electrons move freely at a temperature of around 20,000 degrees Celsius. Although, on the Earth's surface, such heat can be created only in the artificial conditions of a laboratory, *plasmas constitute over ninety-nine percent of*

Bohm's for over twenty years and co-authored *Science, Order, and Creativity* with him.

[4] F. David Peat, *Infinite Potential*, pp. 62-65.

[5] Ibid., p. 65.

> *the matter of the universe—most stars and interstellar gases exist in this fourth state of matter.*[6]

Before proceeding to Bohm's discovery, we need to pause and consider the implications of what has just been stated, and there is no other way to put them, other than to state these implications in the most blunt, naked, and stark fashion possible:

If plasmas constitute ninety-nine percent of all matter in the cosmos, then the physics you and I have been taught and grown up with all our lives—the physics of solids, liquids, gases, of fluid dynamics, of mass and gravity and relativity and black holes and dark matter and all the rest, the physics of Newton and Einstein and Descartes and Leibniz and Galileo and Copernicus and Kepler—*is the physics of only one percent of the cosmos, and thus a very small sub-set of the actual physics of the vast bulk of the cosmos, which is the physics of plasmas*. It thus also means that the physics of electromagnetism and electro-dynamic systems is *far* more fundamental to cosmology than gravity, mass, inertia, and all the trappings of the Newtonian-Einsteinian development will ever be. To be even more blunt and stark about it, it is Tesla, or plasma physicists such as Hannes Alfvén and Anthony Peratt, who are doing "fundamental" physics. To put it yet even *more* bluntly, trying to do cosmological physics on the basis of theories applicable only to the "one percent physics" is a futile enterprise and doomed to failure.

We may now return to what Bohm discovered that both so diverted, and focused, his attention:

> The first theoretical description of a plasma had been given several decades earlier by the chemist Irving Langmuir, but as soon as Bohm began his theoretical study of plasmas

---

[6] Ibid., emphasis added.

> confined within the extremely high magnetic fields of the cyclotron, he discovered some quite unexpected properties in them. Instead of moving freely, for example, the electrons tended to circle around the magnetic field lines.
>
> …
>
> As he studied the plasmas he became struck by their extraordinary nature. They began to take on, for him, the qualities of living beings. *When physicists studied a plasma by introducing an electrical probe, it would generate a charge sheath around the probe and neutralize its effects. It was as if the plasma were protecting itself and preserving its internal status.*[7]

To put this observation somewhat differently, Bohm discovered that plasmas react to the insertion of an electrical probe in the *same* way that the immune systems of organisms – of *life* – react to the presence of a foreign pathogen: they attack it, and isolate it completely from the rest of the organism by encasing it; in the case of a biological organism, the encasement is biological: the pathogen is surrounded by cells and unable to attach to the rest of the organism. In the case of the plasma, the encasement is electro-magnetic. But the response mechanism is virtually identical: plasma responds to such probes like an organism under attack by a foreign object.

Of course, the resemblance of one specific trait common to plasmas and organic life was not enough to convince most scientists that Bohm's suspicions that he was dealing with living beings was correct. And in fact, Bohm was not the first to notice the resemblance of plasmas to biological life, as we shall see.

But it *was* enough to convince some of them to look at other mysterious properties of plasmas, and their more

---

[7] F. David Peat, *Infinite Potential*, pp. 65-66, emphasis added.

mystifying resemblances not only to life, but to intelligent life. However, before we consider what these are, we have to explore the exposition of some of these factors by the "founder" of plasma cosmology, Nobel physics laureate and Swedish physicist Dr. Hannes Alfvén, and by his student and heir to the plasma cosmology tradition, plasma physicist Dr. Anthony Peratt.

Swedish Plasma Physicist Hannes Olof Götsa Alfvén, Ph.D., 1908-1995, 1970 Nobel Laureate in Physics

Dr. Alfvén in later life.

Plasma Physicist Dr. Anthony Peratt, Alfvén's Student and Current Expositor of the Plasma Cosmology Physics

B. A Few Basics of Plasmas: Bounded Extension in Time and Space

Between them, Dr. Alfvén and Dr. Peratt wrote three books that may be reasonably considered the essential textbook introductions not only to plasma physics, but also to its wider implications for physical and even metaphysical cosmology: *Cosmical Electrodynamics* and *Cosmic Plasma*, both by Dr. Alfvén, and *The Physics of the Plasma Universe* by Dr. Peratt. The work of both physicists was also ably summarized for a more general public in Eric J. Lerner's *The*

Big Bang Never Happened, a book which I in turn utilized heavily in my own book *The Cosmic War: Interplanetary Warfare, Modern Physics, and Ancient Texts*.[8]

So what, exactly, do physicists mean when they say plasma? Dr. Peratt spells it out quite clearly right at the beginning of his textbook:

> Plasma consists of electrically charged particles that respond collectively to electromagnetic forces. The charged particles are usually clouds or beams of electrons, ions, and neutrals or a mixture of electrons ions, and neutrals but also can be charged grains or dust particles. Plasma is also created when a gas is brought to a temperature that is comparable to or higher than that in the interior of stars. At these temperatures, all light atoms are stripped of their electrons, and the gas is reduced to its constituent parts: positively charged bare nuclei and negatively charged free electrons. The name plasma is also properly applied to

---

[8] Hannes Alfvén, *Cosmical Electrodynamics* (Oxford: Oxford University Press, 1950, Reprint of the original: ISBN 978-1541348400), and Alfvén, *Cosmic Plasma*, *Astrophysics and Space Science Library*, Volume 82 (Dordrecht, Holland. D. Reidel Publishing Company, 1981. Anthony L. Peratt, *Physics of the Plasma Universe*, 2nd Edition (New York: Springer. 2015. ISBN 978-1-4939-3694-6.) Eric J. Lerner, *The Big Bang Never Happened* (New York: Vintage Books [Random House], 1992, ISBN 978-0-679-74049-X). For my previous discussion of the work of these three men, see my *The Cosmic War: Interplanetary Warfare, Modern Physics, and Ancient Texts* (Kempton, Illinois: Adventures Unlimited Press, 2007, ISBN 978-1-931882-75-0), pp. 28-66. My remarks concerning plasma cosmology in the present book may be considered as revisions and extensions of remarks not only to *The Giza Death Star* books, including *The Giza Death Star Revisited*, but also to *The Cosmic War*.

> ionized gasses at lower temperatures where a considerable fraction of neutral atoms or molecules are present.[9]

Thus, the aurora borealis or aurora australis, ordinary lightning, and even the electrical arcs from arc welders, or the neon gas in a neon sign or fluorescent light bulbs are also plasmas, and as we shall discover later in this chapter, plasmas are also capable of existing inside metals and other types of crystals, and so on.[10] As we shall also discover, it is strongly suspected that the mysterious phenomenon of ball lightning is also a form of plasma.

If one seeks the underlying principle that unites all these seemingly disparate manifestations of "plasma," one must focus on the fact that *they all have in common a kind of "non-atomic" state of matter*, where the electrons of an atom, and its nucleus, exist "apart" from each other, and in a kind of "roaming free"—though as we shall see, not "amorphous"—state. A plasma consisting of uranium or of helium, for example, would have the *electrons* of uranium or helium atoms, and the *nuclei* of uranium or helium atoms, all present in a particular region, but *not* bound together in their familiar state *as* atoms. Or to put it differently, since the matter of the elements comprising a plasma still exist with all their protons, neutrons, and electrons "intact and present" but just not arranged *in atoms*, one may also say that in plasmas, matter exists in a *sub-atomic* or "incomplete atomic" condition.[11]

However, this is not all.

To make matters very much more mysterious and complicated, when one is confronted with other characteristics of plasmas, such as their *extension*, one comes

---

[9] Anthony L. Peratt, *The Physics of the Plasma Universe*, p. 1.

[10] Ibid., p. 2.

[11] Robert Temple, *A New Science of Heaven* (London: Coronet [Hodder and Stoughton, Ltd.], 2021, ISBN 978-1473623743), p. 3.

face to face with an exasperating catalogue of qualities. Consider just the two primary types of extension: (1) in space, and (2) in time. On earth, plasmas may come in forms no bigger than a few microns, all the way up to a few meters, a scale of sizes "spanning six orders of magnitude."[12] But in space, they can fill the vast "void" between the Earth and the Moon, and one plasma structure, the so-called "Sloan Great Wall Filament," is no less than *one billion, three hundred and seventy* ***light years*** *long!*[13] Taking the velocity of light as approximately 186,000 miles per second, that works out to a about 186,000 x 60 x 60 x 24 x 365 x 1.37 x 10^9, or one hundred thirty-three septillion, nine hundred and thirty-three quintillion, and three hundred and ninety-two quadrillion miles—that's

133, 933, 392, 000, 000, 000, 000, 000 miles –

or to put it differently, that's approximately 334,833.5 times the diameter of the Milky Way galaxy, give or take a few score thousand light years! And that's assuming I pecked in all the numbers into my calculator correctly, and I may not have, if one judges from the smoke currently emanating from it.

But calculator melt-down or not, I think the basic point is clear: one is dealing with a structure so vast and so immense that our entire galaxy is as a fly speck.

That, however, is just the enormous spectrum of scales in which plasmas exist *spatially*. What about their extension in time? What are their "lifespans"?

Here again, one is confronted by the fact that on Earth alone they can endure for mere pico-seconds, nano-seconds, or micro-seconds, to "hours, weeks, or years" in the case of

---

[12] Anthony L. Peratt, *The Physics of the Plasma Universe*, p. 3.
[13] Robert Temple, *A New Science of Heaven*, p. 111.

some fluorescent light bulb tubes,[14] and one can only speculate how long the Sloan Great Wall Filament existed prior to its discovery, but for a structure so immense to be observed, and to continue to exist to observation over time suggests a lifetime that might literally be measured in "aeons" or billions of years in order for such a structure even to be formed. Like their extension in space, there is *seemingly* no lower nor upper limit to their extension in time.

With these points in mind, consider following remark, made almost in passing, from Peratt's introduction to plasma physics: "The earth's ionosphere and magnetosphere constitute a cosmic plasma system that is readily available for extensive and detailed in situ observation *and even active experimentation*."[15] As we proceed in this and the following chapter to explore plasma-life hypothesis, the implications of "cosmic plasmas" for the concepts of entanglement, longitudinal waves, superluminal transmission of information, morphogenetic fields, and even weaponization and nuclear detonations, should be borne in mind.

In this light one should consider one well-known area of physics research where plasmas have seemed not only to take on lives of their own, but moreover where they appeared to have stubbornly refused to cooperate with theoretical models and prediction: controlled hot fusion. Under the theory that stars were big hot glowing balls of super-heated hydrogen gas undergoing a constant "chained-up" fusion chain reaction of explosion-contraction (by gravity) fusion-explosion, scientists during the 1950s, after the first "successful" hydrogen bomb tests, proposed that fusion chain reactions were the wave of future energy production, for it would not only be relatively cheap, and clean, lacking the nasty radioactive by-products of

---

[14] Anthony L. Peratt, *The Physics of the Plasma Universe*, p. 3

[15] Anthony L. Peratt, *The Physics of the Plasma Universe*, p. 5, emphasis added.

fission reactors, but also more or less sustainable for as long as the reaction, like the sun, could be contained and sustained. The world would literally never run out of energy. Thus, they reasoned that all one had to do was invent a method of containment of that hot, gassy hydrogen plasma. Since gravity—the means of containment in the models of stars at the time—was not feasible, another means had to be found, and that was electromagnetic containment. It is interesting to note that the earliest designs for fusion reactors date from this period, and with but few "technological refinements" along the way, these designs really have not changed all that much since the 1950s when they were first proposed.

Fusion, and thus a whole new system of energy—and for that matter, since financial systems are based on energy systems, a whole new financial system—was just around the corner. To this day, billions of dollars, euros, reminbi and so on continue to be poured into "big hot fusion" reactors, and we've only managed to sustain reactions of a few seconds. These are always accompanied by headlines announcing—usually with some fanfare—that it is a "breakthrough" and we're on our way to fusion power, but that scientists and engineers still have to work out a few "kinks," or something like that. This has been going on since the 1950s, and still no hot fusion reactors. About all that has been proven by such projects is that they are wonderful ways to launder huge amounts of money for "something else," whatever that may be, even if it is only to keep friends and family gainfully employed in "fusion research."

Except… it did not happen that way. Dr. Alfvén gives an overview of what went wrong:

> The crushing victory of the theoretical approach over the experimental approach lasted only until the theory was used to make experimentally verifiable predictions. From the theory, it was concluded that in the laboratory plasmas

> could easily be confined in magnetic fields and heated to such temperatures as to make thermonuclear release of energy possible. When attempts were made to construct thermonuclear reactors, a confrontation between the theories and reality was unavoidable. The result was catastrophic. Although the theories were generally accepted, the plasma itself refused to believe in them. Instead, the plasma showed a large number of important effects which were not included in the theory. It was slowly realized that one had to develop new theories, but this time in close contact with experiments.
>
> The 'thermonuclear crisis' did not affect cosmic plasma physics very much. The development of the theories continued because they largely dealt with phenomena in regions of space where no real check was possible. The fact that the basis of several of the theories had been proved to be false in the laboratory had very little effect. One said that this did not necessarily prove that they must also be false in the cosmos! Much work was done in developing these theories, leading to a gigantic structure of speculative theories which had no empirical support.[16]

Some of the experimental data that may have been ignored in these early theoretical developments was the clear evidence that plasmas—in the laboratory at least—were not more or less homogeneous. Plasmas, as the chemist Langmuir noted, had a real *structure* and even discrete *regions* within them. We'll return to Langmuir in a moment, for he is crucial to the development of the hypothesis of plasma life.

But it was difficult to view the sun or other stars as anything else but big hot balls of gas or chained up H-bombs, that is to say, it was difficult to view them as anything but a more or less homogeneous nature. Insofar as there was any

---

[16] Hannes Alfvén, *Cosmic Plasma*, p. 2. Notice that Alfvén's diction attributes agency and intention (personality) to plasma!

inhomogeneity in the sun or other stars, it was a difference largely of temperature, and under the chained-up H-bomb model, that was bound to be hotter at the core, gradually cooling toward the surface. Thus, lurking in between the lines of Alfvén's brief review of the "thermonuclear crisis" in plasma physics is the idea that the big chained-up H-bomb model of stellar energy production is simply incorrect.

1. Some Intriguing Pictures of Nuclear Detonations and the Hyper-Dimensional Transduction Hypothesis

By 1945 at least, and earlier if my own hypothesis that the Nazis detonated an atom bomb in October 1944 is correct,[17] scientists had at least *some* strong evidence that plasma fireballs under nuclear reaction conditions are not homogeneous, but exhibit very suggestive manifestations of internal subdivision and structure, as the following pictures from the Trinity test show.

---

[17] See my *Reich of the Black Sun* (Kempton, Illinois: Adventures Unlimited Press, 2005), pp. 1-30ff. If the Nazis did explode an atomic bomb during this time period, then it stands to reason that their scientists, like their American and British counterparts in the Manhattan Project, would have insisted that film of the event be made for use in further study.

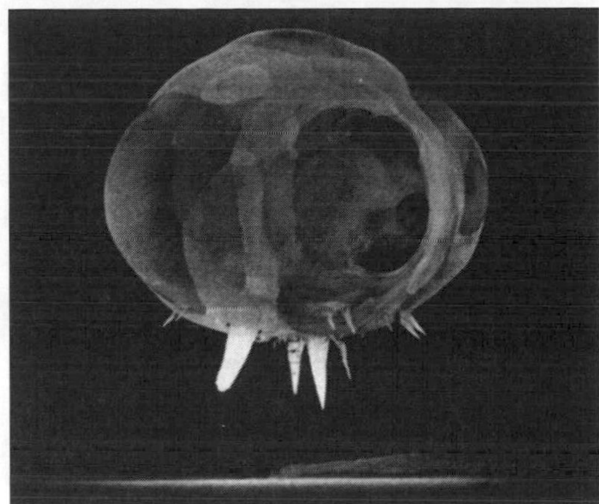

Trinity Test Fireball at detonation.

A negative and enlarged view of the fireball may be more helpful:

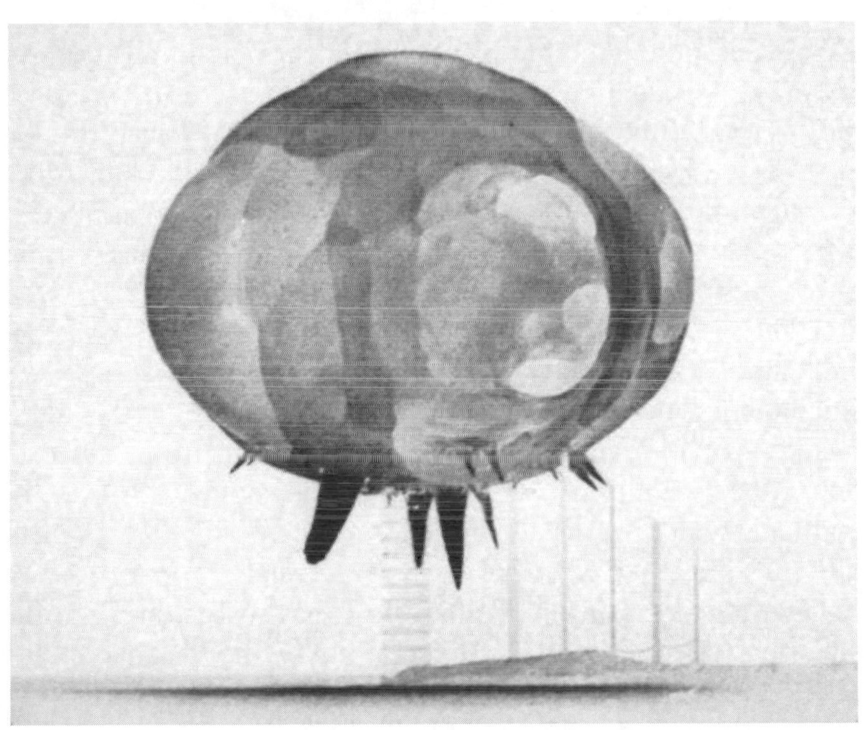

Trinity Test fireball at detonation

When looking at these pictures, note the clear delineations of internal structure in the fireball, including what even looks like an internal toroidal structure on the right, with a void or "vacant" area, or an area of comparatively very low temperature in an otherwise hot plasma. Note also in both pictures the fiery streamers or projections from the fireball to the ground, and, in the negative version of the picture, the vertical lines from the ground up to the fireball. But notice something else. If one did not already know that these pictures were of the moment of the detonation of the Trinity test, one might have thought one was looking at the picture of a living cell, taken from a microscope.

In any case, I believe these streamers and filaments—about which *much* more is to come later—are a profound clue as to what may be taking place in nuclear reactions, and why yields of the same basic designs of bombs seem to vary with the time and place of detonation. They are also a profound clue as to why the sun is not simply a big chained-up hydrogen bomb. For years I've been maintaining that nuclear bombs, for a brief moment, act as transducers of energy from the local structure of spacetime, a structure which, moreover, is a lattice or crystalline structure.[18] In other words, nuclear and thermonuclear bombs are *hyper-dimensional devices*, since there is another source of energy than just the fission or fusion reaction, another source which comes from, and can only be modeled *by*, hyper-dimensional kinds of mathematics…

…a source like *electromagnetism, electricity, and plasma.*

The streamers in the fireball, in other words, are like the electrical streamers that are sent out by the plasma in the

[18] See for example, my *Grid of the Gods: The Aftermath of the Cosmic War and the Physics of the Pyramid Peoples* (Kempton, Illinois: Adventures Unlimited Press, 2011), pp. 1-36.

cumulo-nimbus clouds during a thunderstorm, seeking out a pathway prior to a lightning strike. The streamers coming *from the fireball to the ground, and up from the ground to the fireball, indicate flows of electromagnetic, electrostatic energy in the reaction.*

Or to put all this *as simply as possible:* if one sets off a nuclear bomb in the atmosphere or ionosphere, one is creating *a (hot)plasma inside a (cold) plasma* and thus energy will flow between the two, depending on heat, charge, magnetic field, and other conditions. That energy may in turn also depend on the harmonic relationships between the two. The bomb, in other words, is also a *circuit*, and part of a much *larger* circuit. This view, as we shall see later in this chapter, is a profound clue as to what is really going on in stars, and why they're not just, or even primarily, big chained-up h-bombs.

These two pictures, in other words, alone suggest little-appreciated—or at least, little *commented* upon—electro-dynamic aspects to nuclear detonations, and it is the presence of this factor which may explain why early calculations of bomb yields were so often wide of the mark, and in the infamous cases of the Castle Bravo and Castle Koon tests, disastrously so. This *is* the hyper-dimensional source of that transduced energy, for as the famous electrical engineer and theoretician Gabriel Kron pointed out, all electrical circuits are hyper-dimensional devices, because one simply cannot explain any electrical circuit without the use of imaginary, or "hyper-dimensional," numbers. And as for local lattice structure, we shall discover later in this chapter that plasmas bear a remarkable resemblance to, and affinity for, crystals.[19]

---

[19] And for those who have read my other books and been on this journey with me all these years, the Nazi scientist working for Juan Peron, Dr. Ronald Richter, also viewed plasmas as transducers of a "cell structure" in space-time, which he in turn

In any case, there are other pictures from the Trinity test that also show internal structure to the plasma fireball, as the picture on the next page illustrates.

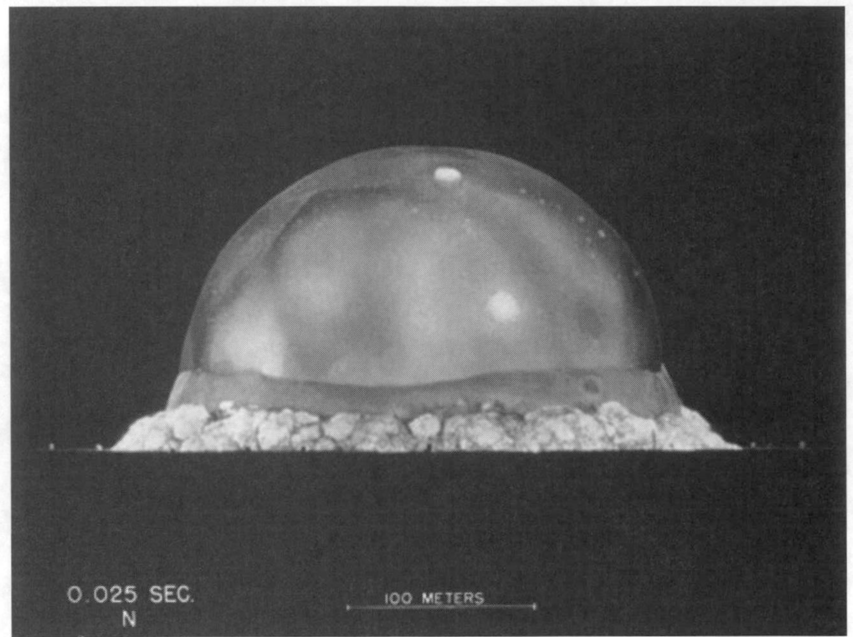

Trinity Test at .025 Seconds

If the plasmas of nuclear fireballs are momentarily gating energy from the local lattice structure of space-time—or if one wishes to view it in "Tesla" or "Gabriel Kron" terms, the

---

called "zero point energy." And of course, the Nazi Bell technology was an unusual twist—pun intended—to a standard plasma focus, in that the Nazis his upon the rather brilliant idea of electrically and mechanically counter-rotating a *plasma* in the device, as I've outlined in my books *The SS Brotherhood of the Bell*, *Secrets of the Unified Field, The Philosophers' Stone* and *The Nazi International*.

local "circuit geometry parameters"[20]—then what about explosions in the upper atmosphere, in the near-vacuum of space? Do they show similar evidence of "gating" as the Trinity photographs possibly do?

The answer is provided by a series of films that were taken during the 1962 atmospheric tests called Operation Fishbowl, a set of high atmospheric and ionospheric tests that were conducted as part of Operation Dominic. These tests were conducted by the USA in response to the Soviet Union's atmospheric detonation of its massive 57 megaton "Tsar Bomba" in October of 1961, a test this author remembers as a boy (and an angry Adlai Stephenson talking about it on the CBS Evening News)! The following still frames (and negatives) were taken from films of these tests, and they show clearly and conclusively yet another version of these streamers or filaments:

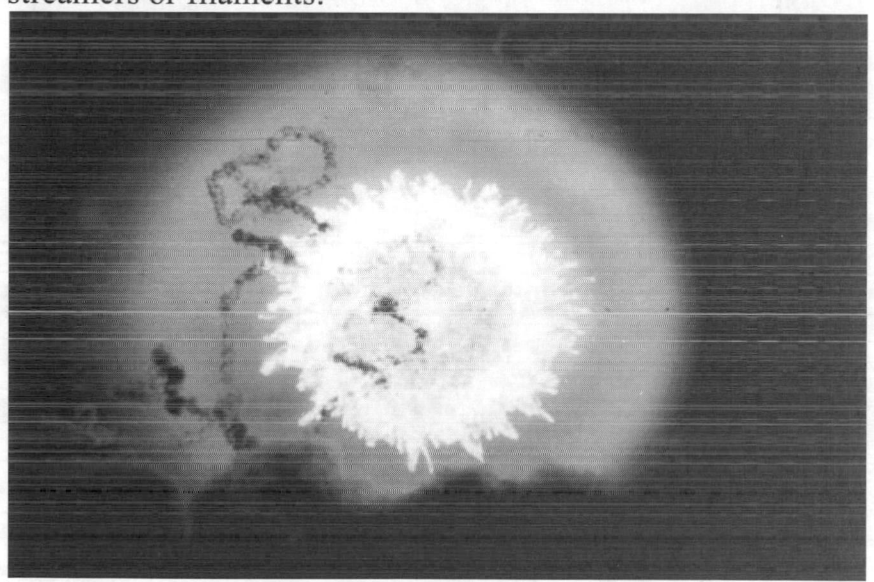

Operation Fishbowl Detonation, 1962

---

[20] See my *Giza Death Star Revisited* (Kempton, Illinois: Adventures Unlimited Press, 2023), pp. 201-202.

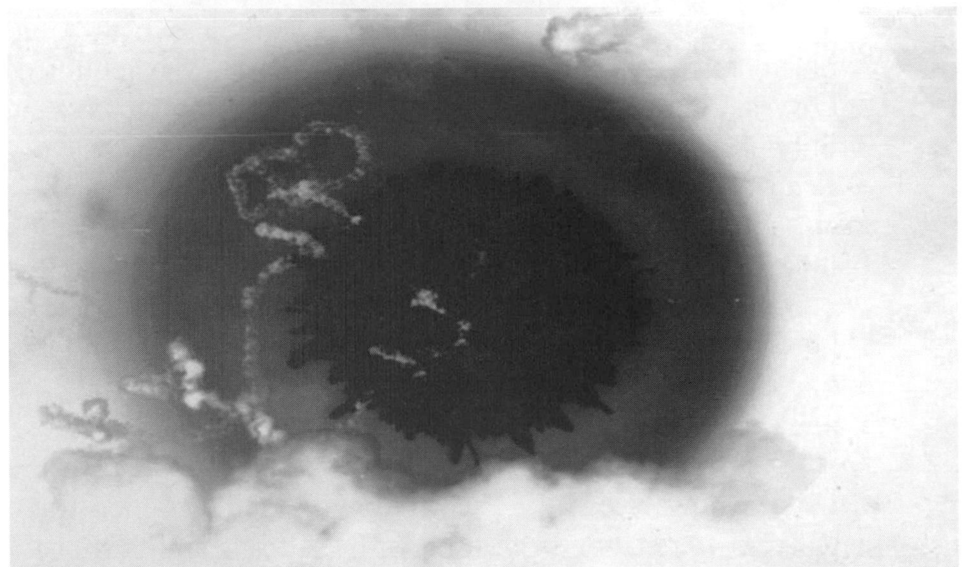

Operation Fishbowl Detonation 1962, Negative: the darkest region represents the hottest, white represents cooler regions. Notice the white filaments near the detonation.

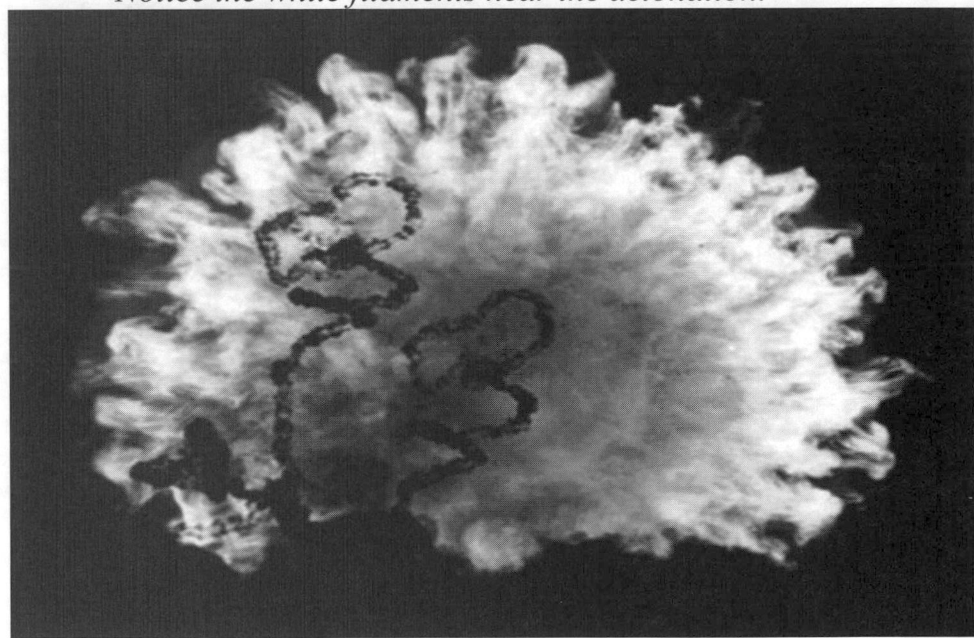

Another Operation Fishbowl Detonation (1962);

Note again the structure in the fireball, and the dark filamentary streamers

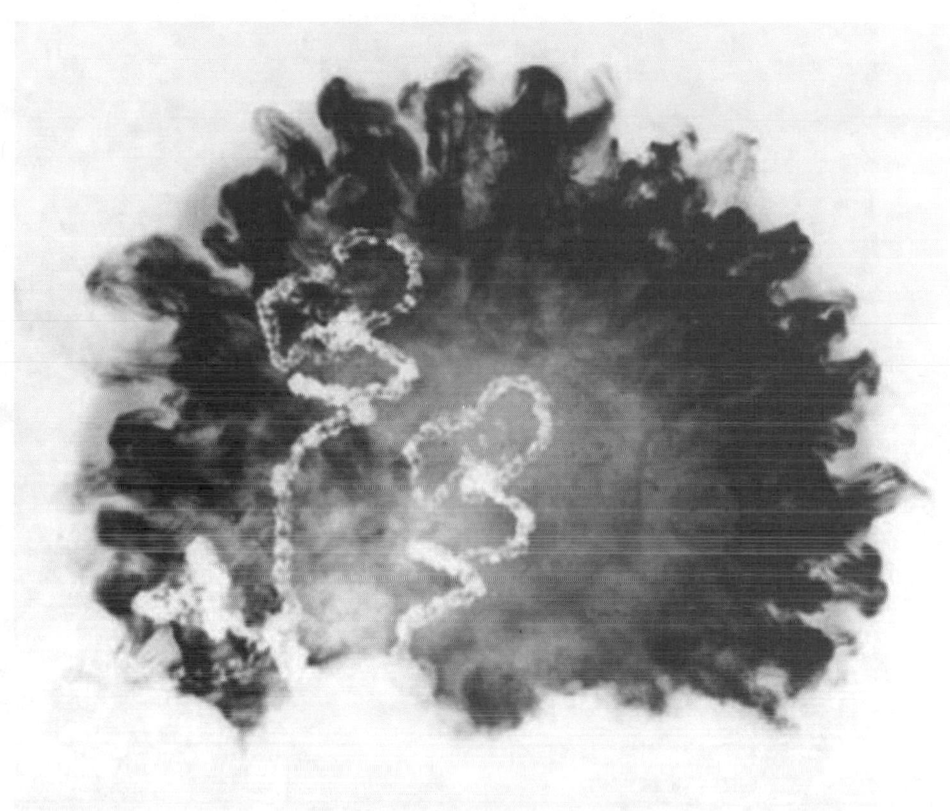

Another negative view of the same Operation Fishbowl Detonation, with the filamentary streamers in white

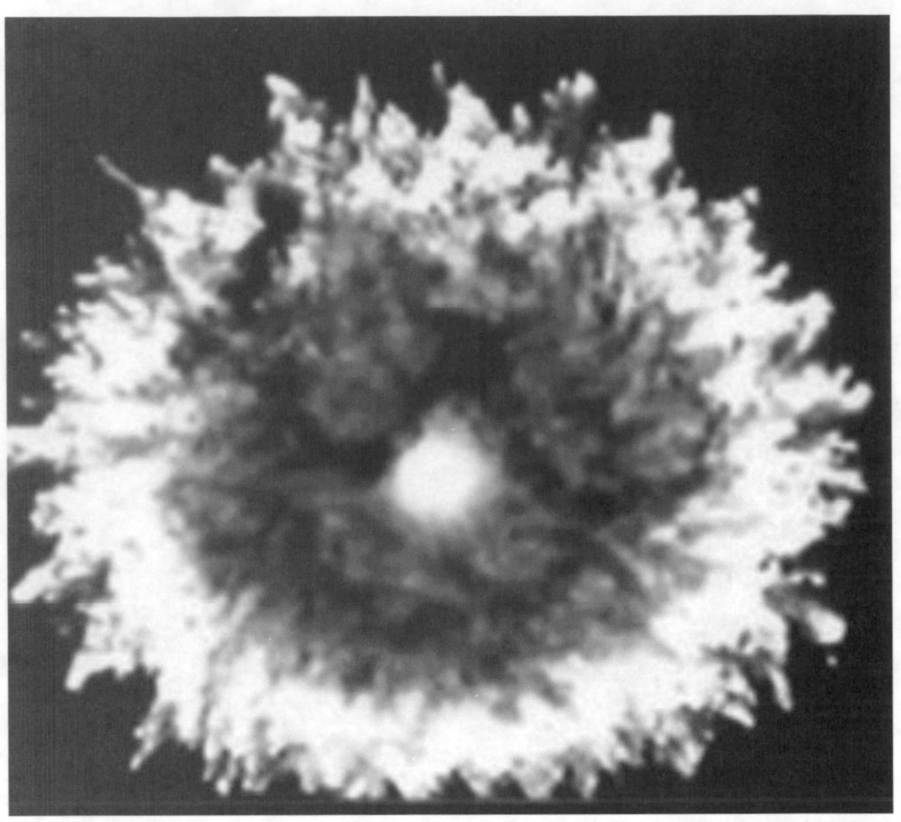

Another Operation Fishbowl Detonation at the moment of detonation. Note again the internal structure of the plasma fireball, including the dark filamentary streamer

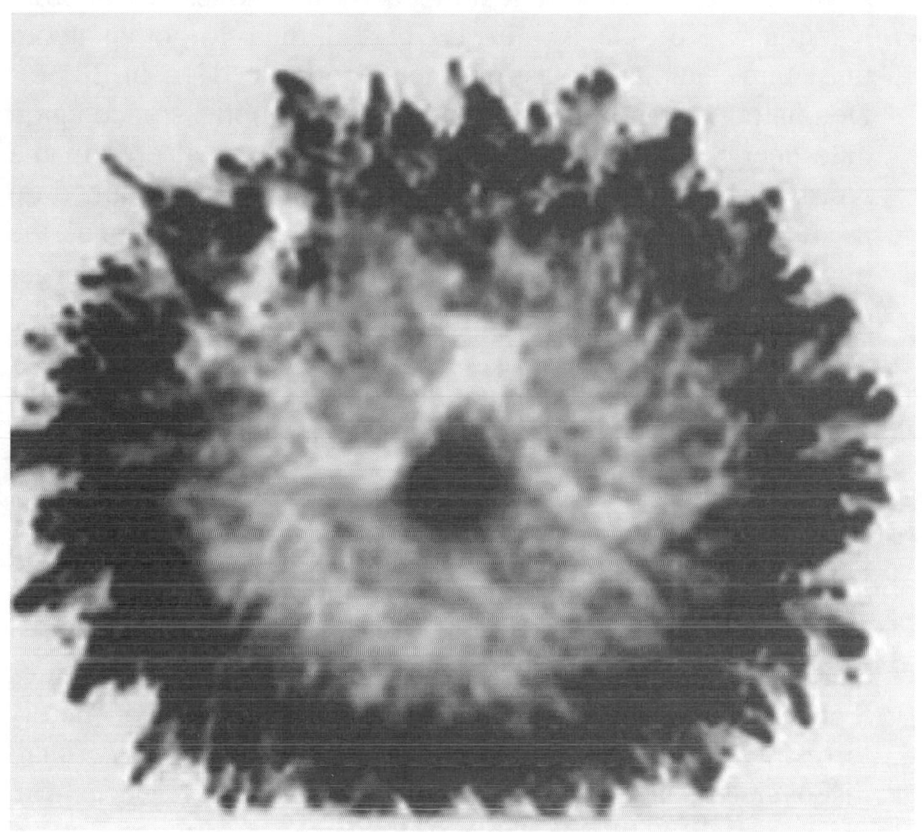

The Same Operation Fishbowl Detonation in Negative view, with the filamentary streamer in white.

What might happen, though, if a nuclear bomb were detonated not even in the ultra-thin upper atmosphere of the Earth, but in the vacant space between the Earth and the Moon? Or for that matter, in the "Sloan Great Wall?"

The very same thing, and then some, might happen, and for two reasons: (1) the solar wind of particles streaming from the Sun, and (2) the ultra-thin Kordylewski cloud that exists between the Earth and the Moon. This very thin "dust plasma" is an endothermic plasma that exists between the Earth and the Moon, first noticed by the Polish astronomer Kazimierz Kordylewski in 1961, and then forgotten about until three Hungarian astronomers "re-noticed" it in 2019.[21] Detonating a bomb in this cloud would doubtless once again gate energy not only from the solar wind but also from the Kordylewski cloud, energy beyond that of what is chained up in the uranium, plutonium, or deuterium and tritium of the bomb fuel. Again, the bomb is only *part* of a much larger circuit.

a. An Excursion into the Farrell Corollaries to the Kardashev Scale: A MAD Cosmos

The possibility that nuclear plasmas are transducing energy from the surrounding plasma environment raises once again my hypothesis of the Farrell Corollaries to the Kardashev Scale of Civilization Types, and to the possibilities that nuclear testing may be a kind of cosmic, and not merely terrestrial, gunboat diplomacy and saber-rattling. We shall discover later in this chapter very suggestive evidence from the Sun itself that this is the case.

For the moment, however, we assume that under certain specific conditions a thermonuclear detonation would transduce energy from the plasma environment in which it is detonated. And let us assume that this plasma environment was that of a plasma of galactic scale or extent.

In the Kardashev Classification system of Civilizational Types, a Class One Civilization requires *the energy consumption* of an entire planet to sustain itself. In a Class Two Civilization, the energy consumption needed to sustain the civilization jumps up to an entire star, and at the summit

---

[21] Robert Temple, *A New Science of Heaven*, p. 2.

of civilizational achievement, the Class Three Civilization, the energy consumption jumps to that of an entire galaxy.

In my hypothesized corollaries, I assumed that if one were trying to convince a Civilization of Class One or Two to leave humanity "well enough alone," that in the absence of the need to consume entire planets or stars in order to sustain our civilization, we would have to demonstrate to such Civilizations our ability to engineer systems *of planetary or stellar scale*, such as weather in the case of planets, or solar winds—a form of *plasma*—from stars. The ability to engineer such systems implies the ability to weaponize them. From what has been hypothesized about nuclear detonation plasmas transducing energy from a plasma environment, one may extend those corollaries to plasmas of planetary, stellar-system, or galactic-system scale. *Plasmas* constitute the unifying factor to engineering systems of all three scales, and hence become a means of "gunboat diplomacy"—provided those laws of transduction can be learned—even with Type Three Civilizations.

b. Back to the Plasma Life Hypothesis

However, what does any of this, and particularly nuclear and thermonuclear explosions, have to do with the hypothesis that plasmas—or at least, *some* of them—may be inorganic life forms?

The answer has to do with their internal *structure* and *behavior*. The biggest clue lies in the term "plasma" itself to describe this strange state of matter in which all the sub-atomic particles of an element or chemical compound are there, but *not* arranged into atoms. The term plasma is, obviously, a biological and *medical* term. It was applied to this state of matter by the American 1932 Nobel Laureate in Chemistry, Irving Langmuir, because of the way plasmas consisted of electrons and ions reminded him of blood, and thus, of living systems! In other words, the very term was applied to the phenomenon because a famous chemist noticed a resemblance to life![22]

2. The Physics of the One Percent and the Ninety-Nine Percent

a. Cosmological Physics as Biophysics

As nothing else can, this brief excursion into nuclear and thermonuclear detonations highlights a principal difficulty of the plasma-life hypothesis, for if some plasmas are actual inorganic life forms, and some of *these* in turn are possibly intelligent, then what *of* the nuclear and thermonuclear plasmas of bombs and stars? How does one tell which is which?

We shall propose some tentative solutions for this dilemma later in this chapter, but for the present, we must pause to take stock of the implications of the hypothesis thus far.

We have already observed that plasma constitutes approximately ninety-nine percent of all matter in the universe. The other one percent—the gases, liquids, and solids with which we are most familiar—constitute the principal *subject matter* of most physics from Euclid to Einstein. *That* physics has led to the "gravity-relativity-big bang" cosmology that most of us tend to think of when (and if!) we think of cosmological physics at all.

Robert Temple puts the difference between the "one percent" physics and the "ninety-nine percent" physics very aptly and elegantly:

---

[22] Ibid., p. 16.

> Instead of trying to model the Universe on the basis of the very rare and specialized form of dense matter found on our planet, we need to treat dense 'physical matter' as an exceptional form of the true 'universal matter', plasma. There is no use in our trying to establish universal laws on the basis of a tiny sample of far less than one percent of what exists. We need to establish physical laws on the basis of plasma and specify what we call 'physical matter' as a very special and limited case, which has no justification for being used as a basis for describing the majority of constituents of the Universe.
>
> So drastic does our rearrangement of science need to be that we can take our present physics, shrink it and plonk it into a tiny corner of the representation of the wider truth, where it can describe those minority conditions appertaining to planets and other such 'solid' bodies, as a kind of footnote or addendum to a true universal science.[23]

Consequently, if plasma constitutes most of the matter of the universe, then the physics we have been doing thus far has been the physics of "the one percent," *and if some plasmas are indeed a form of inorganic life, and some of that in turn is possibly intelligent life*, then this also means that the physics of the ninety-nine precent is a kind of "biophysics," and that it is also a kind of "consciousness physics" as well.

From this point onward throughout the rest of this book, and for the sake of argument and exploration of the full implication of the plasma-life hypothesis, we shall assume that it is true, and that some plasmas are not only alive, but also intelligent. Along the way, we shall explore data that suggestively buttress this hypothesis. We shall, in short, give free rein to the imagination to explore those implications.

b, The Profound Implication for Textual Interpretation

---

[23] Robert Temple, *A New Science of Heaven*, p. 45.

and Specific Types of Events Since the End of World War Two

As soon as we *do* give free rein to the imagination to explore the implications of the plasma life hypothesis, we are confronted by its profound implication for the interpretation of texts, and particularly those dealing with the "wars of gods and men."

For example, in my book *The Cosmic War* I pointed out that for certain proponents of the plasma universe (or the electric universe theory, as it is sometimes also known), the "wars of gods and men" spoken of in ancient texts from the Graeco-Roman or Mesopotamian worlds to India or Meso-America are *metaphors for electrical arcing* between planets in the solar system.

But the plasma life hypothesis turns the whole metaphor on its head, for if as we saw in the previous chapter angels (and demons) have charge over specific planets or regions of planets on the one hand, and they in turn are living inorganic intelligence beings, then the "wars" are no longer mere metaphors designating arcing between planets. They *remain that, but become much more: they become the intentional acts of destruction of intelligent and very powerful beings*.

The war, in other words, is no longer *metaphorical*, but very *real*, and *very* cosmic. Noting that some ancient texts refer to angels as lights, Robert Temple observes the very same implication with respect to the interpretation of texts if the plasma life hypothesis is true:

> However, it is not only the good entities, but also the bad entities who reside in luminous clouds. The Gnostic name for the Devil is the Chief Archon, also called Samael, Yaldabaoth, and Saklas (which means 'the Fool'). The *(Apocryphon of John*) tells us that the Chief Archon 'created for himself an Aeon (a special place) that burns with a luminous fire, the one in which he exists now'. (The

> Gnostics altered the meaning of the ancient Greek word *aion* and used it in their own peculiar way. The term 'Aeon', the Latin form that we use in English, occurs constantly in their texts.)
>
> In other words, the Devil himself lives in a fiery plasma cloud. So consequently, both the powers of Good and the powers of Evil dwell in or consist of plasma clouds. *The War in Heaven is thus a war between good and bad plasmas,* and the extent to which they can recruit humans on their respective sides is assumed to have a bearing on how long the world will last before it reaches its ultimate climax when the final reckoning occurs.[24]

The explanatory power of the plasma life hypothesis is thus profoundly broad and deep at one and the same time.

As Temple also notes, and as we saw in the previous chapter in our examination of St. John of Damascus' strange

---

[24] Robert Temple, *A New Science of Heaven*, p. 74, emphasis added. I believe Temple has overstated the use of the term αιων here, in order to underscore his (quite correct) point that Gnostics often use common terms in a peculiar way, in this case, as a kind of "special place." Αιων is usually translated as an "age," and in a way very similar to the Hindu notion of various "ages" or "yugas," the αιων thus designates an overarching pattern of a culture or "world" whose existence endures for a prolonged period of time, usually several millennia. An "age" or aeon in this sense comes to mean a "world" or cultural context. This idea of ages occurs in the Greek version of Christian doxologies as the phrase "unto ages of ages," a poetic metaphor meaning a prolonged and unlimited extension in time. Its Latin version, *saecula saeculorum* is a literal translation also meaning "ages of ages," but its standard liturgical English translation, "world without end" is meant to designate not the *temporal* aspect of an age or aeon/αιων, but the *blessed condition or "cultural state,"* which is also bound up in the term αιων.

and openly contradictory language regarding angels, the word "spiritual" in many contexts might refer to plasma,[25] a kind of super-fine matter filling the vastness of "not-quite-empty" space. For the Damascene, it was a kind of matter that was immaterial with respect to man, but material with respect to God. Had he known Michael Faraday or James Clerk Maxwell, he might have referred to it as *aether lumeniferous*, or had he known Irving Langmuir, as plasma.

3. Characteristics of Life

As we continue to peel away the various layers of the plasma life hypothesis, we have arrived at that place where we must begin to ponder more specific cases of life, and of plasmas. We do so in part to clarify a point; we are not arguing that all plasmas *are* a form of inorganic life, only that *some* of them may be, and of these only that *some* may be intelligent. The question thus becomes, how would one delineate between these categories? What tests would one apply or what characteristics would be involved in each? We will eventually return to these questions and propose some simple (and perhaps even simplistic) ideas in answer to each.

For the present, however, we need to consider a few of the hallmarks of organic life as we know it in order to appreciate the strange analogues between each of them, and their "plasma versions." In short, it is because of the analogues to each of the following that more and more people are beginning to entertain the hypothesis that plasmas—or at least some of them—might be a kind of inorganic life, and that some of them might even be intelligent.

1) All life as we know it involves *the consumption and conversion of food for energy*;

[25] Robert Temple, *A New Science of Heaven*, p. 6.

2) All life as we know it *is thus bounded and of specific extension, and composed of membranes delineating certain interior regions—and* ***voids or empty spaces****—which perform specific functions including that of consumption and conversion of food; i.e., all life has a* ***body****;* to put this country simple: all life as we know it is at its most basic topological level, a *tube*, consisting of a membrane and a hole. From earthworm to elephant or grub to gorilla, all life forms are but variations on the theme of "tube."
3) All life as we know it also *evacuates or eliminates waste* (yet another variation on the theme of *tube*);
4) All life as we know it also *reproduces;* and combining items 3 and 4:
5) All life has means of projecting matter and energy *outside* of itself;
6) All life has means *of sensing and responding to its environment*, which in intelligent life means the ability also to communicate via a variety of signs, sounds, smells, and (particularly in the case of intelligent life) symbols; and,
7) All life has or displays *some* type of mobility; and finally,
8) All life has some type of *memory*, which is particularly true of intelligent life and its ability to process and reason by the manipulation of symbols.

Of course, some would dispute this or that aspect of this list, adding a point here or subtracting a point there. The overall effect, however, remains the same, and with that, we turn to the consideration of some specific, little known and oftentimes astonishing facts of plasmas. These facts may be reduced to two phenomena, filaments, and "sheaths" or "sheets." When one looks at these and compares them to the eight points in this list, it becomes much clearer why some scientists suspect that they might be dealing with a very different type of life form.

C. Filaments, Plasma Pinches, and Helixes; Information and Observation, Memory, Communications, Consumption, and Evacuation

Hannes Alfvén notes the following at the beginning of his introduction to plasma cosmology:

> … (As) soon as an *electric current* is passed through a quiescent plasma, a number of complicated phenomena are produced which require an extensive development of classical theory, sometimes even a new approach.
>
> The most important of these 'anomalous' properties are:
>
> (a) Sometimes the plasma becomes more '*noisy*' than theoretically expected.
>
> (b) The *energy distribution* becomes strongly *non-Maxwellian*; there is a considerable, sometimes extremely large, excess of high energy particles. The velocity distribution is very often highly anistropic (sic).
>
> (c) The *electron temperature* may be orders of magnitude larger than the *ion temperature*, which may be substantially higher than the *neutral gas temperature*, which again may differ from the temperature of the electrodes and the walls of the discharge tube or the temperature of the dust (in case the plasma is 'dusty'…). Certainly this can be accounted for by classical theory; but astrophysical plasmas are often treated as if the mentioned temperatures were necessarily equal.

> Further, there are a very large number of phenomena which are referred to as 'instabilities'…. Examples of such phenomena are:
>
> (d) At sufficiently *large current density*, the plasma may contract into *filaments*…
>
> (e) In case the plasma consists of a *gas mixture,* the components often *separate*… [26]

There are two important points to take from this passage. Firstly, observe that *under conditions of electrical stress*, plasmas exhibit high anisotropy (inequality) of temperature distribution. *Free electron* regions in plasmas may be many orders of magnitude hotter than regions of positive ions, and all this in turn is again hotter than an ordinary gas of the same elements or compounds. Secondly, if the density of electrical current in such circumstances is big enough, the plasma will contract or pinch into *filaments or streamers of current*, such as we observed in the pictures of the Operation Fishbowl nuclear fireballs. Under even more special conditions where currents in plasmas are parallel to each other, they will pinch together into a *helical* filamentary structure.

And again, under other special conditions of resistance and inductance, Alfvén notes that an explosion can occur dependent on these parameters of the circuit's resistance and inductance, almost exactly as Nikola Tesla observed almost a century earlier during his Colorado Springs electrical impulse experiments. This explosion occurs in what is called a "double layer," about which more in a moment.

For the present, however, we must take note of yet another statement in Alfvén's text whose implications will be immediately obvious when considered in connection to the previous discussion on nuclear detonations:

---

[26] Hannes Alfvén, *Cosmic Plasma*, p.8, emphasis in the original.

> ...(In) cosmic plasmas the perhaps most important construction mechanism is the *electromagnetic attraction* between parallel currents. A manifestation of this mechanism is the *pinch effect*, which was studied by Bennett long ago (134) and has received much attention in connection with thermonuclear research. As we shall see, phenomena of this general type also exist on a cosmic scale, and lead to a bunching of currents and magnetic fields to filaments or 'magnetic ropes'. This bunching is usually accompanied by an accumulation of matter, and it may explain the observational fact that cosmic matter exhibits an abundance of *filamentary structures*... This same mechanism may also evacuate the regions near the rope and produce regions of exceptionally low densities...[27]

Many implications fall out from careful consideration of these two passages, but they may not be immediately apparent unless we consider just one practical implication and application: tornadoes and hurricanes.

The typical meteorological explanation of these terribly violent vorticular storms is that they are caused when masses of hot moist air get trapped below layers of cold dry air. The hot air naturally wants to rise, and the cold air naturally wants to fall, and thus the vortex is born as the hot air circles up, and the cold air rushes down elsewhere.

But it is much more likely that the vorticular storm itself is a *pinched helical filament* brought about by the charge differentials in a violent storm and the plasma conditions that constitute such storms. The vortex, in other words, is the result primarily of *electrical and magnetic*, not *thermal*,

---

[27] Hannes Alfvén, *Cosmic Plasma*, p. 22, emphases in the original.

conditions.[28] The thermal conditions may amplify the effect, but they are not its primary cause. As per the dictum of Hungarian electrical engineer Gabriel Kron, once we say "electrical" we are also saying "hyper-dimensional," and thus the "plasma environment" of such storms would account for the strange anomalies often found in their wake, e.g., blades of grass or hay, or even a vinyl record or compact disc, embedded in tree trunks,[29] anomalies which may be signs or symptoms of a brief dimensional collapse as much as they are of an object being drilled into another by tremendous force or wind. The plasma-filamentary nature of such storms may be indicated by the reports of some eyewitnesses of tornadoes who have reported seeing electrical arcing inside the funnel as it has passed over them.[30] Once one has reached this conclusion, then with the correct circuit parameters and plasma conditions, it becomes possible to produce and steer such storms.[31]

The importance of these filaments and their helical structure cannot be overemphasized, for in a certain sense, as conductors of current, they may function quite literally in a manner similar to tubes in organic life, i.e., as a means of intake—and expulsion—of "food" or energy. Indeed, the "double helix" structure of some plasma filaments is one of the principal reasons that some thinkers and biologists suspect that plasmas might be an inorganic life form, given their resemblance to DNA double helixes. Robert Temple notes that

---

[28] See my *Covert Wars and Breakaway Civilizations: The Secret Space Program, Clestial Psyops, and Hidden Conflicts*, pp. 227-242.

[29] Joseph P. Farrell, *Covert Wars and Breakaway Civilizations,* p. 229.

[30] Ibid., pp. 234-235.

[31] Ibid., p. 238.

> since the 1970s there have been cell biologists insisting that charged currents flow along the DNA molecules inside our bodies, and that they are superconducting. Double helixes not only carry currents, they transmit information. All of this is getting us closer and closer to what I believe to be the nature and structure of a plasma body, and to the reasons for believing that intelligence can evolve in plasma.[32]

In other words, organic life forms themselves involve plasma phenomena, not the least of which may be the DNA double helix itself, whose helical structure in turn may be the result or manifestation of an underlying electrical plasma pinch effect.

The implications are obvious, and enormous, not the least for the question of "extraterrestrial life," for by the nature of the case, one is dealing with possible life forms that are of vast extent in time and space, that are effectively "bodiless" as compared to organic life, but—if it is intelligent on top of everything else—of such long memory, intelligence, and therefore power that the ancient wars of Gods and men, and their divine "thunderbolts" finally begin to make sense. To an intelligent being of the spatial size and temporal memory and extent of the Sloan Great Wall, the destruction of a mere planet or stellar system would be as the crater left in the ground by the explosion of an artillery projectile is to us. "After all," says Robert Temple,

> Who needs little green men when you've got gigantic intelligent clouds on your doorstep, which are billions of times more intelligent than any little green men could ever be, billions of years older than any possible organic life

---

[32] Robert Temple, *A New Science of Heaven*, p. 111.

> form, and the entities who must in effect be the true Masters of the Universe?[33]

These considerations lie behind the extension of the plasma life hypothesis to include *intelligent* life.

They may be summarized in three basic points; plasmas *may* be intelligent inorganic life forms because:

1) they can be found to incorporate or produce double helical structures, and hence have an aperiodical crystalline form, ideal for the storage and transmission of *information*; in other words, the structure might account for both an information storage and retrieval as well as communications or conveyance system;
2) their great extent in space, and
3) their great extent in time also gives them access to extremely long memory based on a vast experience, or, if one prefer, "database."

We shall have more to say about these implications for "intelligent inorganic" and "non-atomic" life when we ponder other details of plasmas such as ball lightning, but for the moment, we must consider yet another fundamental feature of plasmas under electrical stress: sheaths, membranes, or "double layers."

D. Sheaths, Membranes, Regions, Organs, Voids, Cells, and Crystals

"Double layers" in plasmas are a kind of "electrostatic structure"[34] that constitute the analogue of "membranes" in

---

[33] Robert Temple, *A New Science of Heaven*, p. 35.

[34] Anthony L. Peratt, *The Physics of the Plasma Universe*, p. 175.

organic life, in that they distinguish discrete regions within plasmas, regions differing in charge, temperature, composition and so on. The *formation* of double layers in plasmas moreover strongly resembles the types of immune-responses of organic life forms in that these double layers are formed often in response to the insertion of electrodes, and they can also form as a protective layer against walls and other barriers. Alfvén states the following in respect to the phenomenon:

> In a low density plasma, localized space charge regions may build up large potential drops over distances… Such regions have been called *electric double layers*. An electric double layer is the simplest space charge distribution that gives a potential drop in the layer and a vanishing electric field on each side of the layer… In the laboratory, double layers have been studied for half a century, but their importance in cosmic plasmas has not been generally recognized until recently. A number of investigations have confirmed the existence of double layers under various conditions, both in the laboratory and in the magnetosphere….
>
> Double layers may be produced in a number of ways. **In general, a plasma screens itself from walls and electrodes by producing double layers, which in this case often are referred to as *sheaths*. In addition, if the electron temperature, for example, is different in two regions of the plasma, the transition between them is often not smooth. Instead, the plasma divides itself in two (or several) homogeneous regions, separated by one (or several) double layers.**[35]

But double layers also do something else:

---

[35] Hannes Alfvén, *Cosmic Plasma*, p. 29, boldface emphasis added, italicized emphasis in the original.

> A double layer is usually *noisy*; in other words, it produces oscillations within a large frequency band. Often the amplitude of the noise is small compared to the voltage drop across the double layer, and this can be considered as (almost) static… However, a double layer may also become unstable and *explode*, by which we mean that the voltage drop suddenly increases by orders of magnitude…. The character of the explosion is largely determined by the inductance L and the resistance R of the circuit in which the current flows.[36]

And, again echoing Nikola Tesla's discovery that circuit parameters and segmentation amplify the electro-acoustic shockwave effect, Alfvén notes how *he* discovered the same phenomenon under slightly different circumstances a few decades after Tesla:

> (Exploding double layers were first discovered and studied in mercury rectifiers used in d.c. high-power transmission circuits.)[37]

And lest anyone miss the cosmic implications of the discovery, he adds:

> The phenomenon is likely to be basic for the understanding of solar flares, magnetic substorms and related phenomena.[38]

---

[36] Hannes Alfvén., p. 30

[37] Ibid.

[38] Ibid. For Alfvén's work with the plasmas of mercury rectifiers, see my *The Cosmic War: Interlanetary Warfare, Modern Physics and Ancient Texts*, pp. 28-39, especially pp. 33-39.

Note what Alfvén has actually said: these double layers within plasmas are not only "electrostatic structures," but they are electro-acoustic *membranes* that respond over a wide range of frequencies. They act, in other words, as resonators of such waves, and thus, as acoustic resonators, they respond like all such resonators do when they cannot damp the energy being loaded into them fast enough: they collapse and explode. In the next chapter we shall see how this applies to the weapon hypothesis of the Great Pyramid.

For the remainder of the present chapter, however, we must look more closely at three phenomena in relation to filaments and double layers by again reconsidering the "big chained up hydrogen bomb" model of stars, the problem of ball lightning and its strange behavior, and the problem of "ambiplasmas."

1. "Food," "Breathing," and Great Balls of Fire

Plasma cosmology both proposed the big chained-up h-bomb model of stars (after all, the sun is said to be a hot glowing ball of thermonuclear plasma in a perpetual state of gravity-restrained explosion), highlighted its massive (and little known) problems, and posits a resolution—though a somewhat disturbing one—all at the same time. To come straight to the point, on the model of the gravitationally-chained-up-H-bomb model of stars, it is impossible that the reaction should ever end. If it ends, the star in question either explodes in a gigantic nova or super-nova, or runs out of fuel, sputters and coughs a bit, and dies. In some of these "sputtering and coughing" models, the remaining matter of the star collapses into a super-cooled super-dense matter and becomes a neutron star, a cubic half-inch of which would weigh several times the mass of the Earth. This would warp local space tremendously, thus compressing the remaining matter even more, until, in some models, the result is a black hole.

All this from chained-up H-bombs! Wholesale dividends of speculation from a minimum investment of tensors!

Except that there's a small problem that cannot be explained on the chained-up H-bomb model... *at all.*

One difficulty that the chained-up H-bomb model recently encountered is that the further towards the core of the Sun one goes, the *cooler* it apparently is. In fact, the photosphere of the Sun, i.e., its actual surface, is a few thousand degrees centigrade, whereas the corona, much farther from the Sun's supposed thermonuclear reactor core than the photosphere, is actually in the millions of degrees centigrade of heat, i.e., at least three orders of magnitude hotter.[39]

The *real* problems begin when one considers the constant stream of energy and particles emanating from the Sun, a stream that has been more or less continuous for approximately four billion years.

"More or less continuous" are the key words here, because as Robert Temple has noted,

> In May of 1999, a very strange thing happened. *For two days, the solar wind stopped completely.* That certainly poses some problems for conventional ideas about the Sun. Did somebody turn off the central bomb? *How can you turn off a thermonuclear explosion and then start it up again two days later?*[40]

[39] Robert Temple, *A New Science of Heaven*, pp. 122ff.

[40] Robert Temple, *A New Science of Heaven*, p. 125, emphasis added. Q.v. also "The Day the Solar Wind Disappeared," science.nasa.gov/science-news/science-at-nasa/199/ast13dec99_1.

As if this were not enough, there is the little problem of the "solar breathing" cycle, yet another anomalous bit of data for the chained-up-H-bomb theory, for

> …every 2 minutes and 40 seconds, the Sun shrinks in size and re-expands, or in other words rises and falls, by six miles. That's a long way to fall and a fast rise! There is no 'orthodox' explanation for this strange fact. Is the Sun breathing? If there were continual pressure from a thermonuclear explosion at the core of the Sun, how could that pressure 'breath' every two minutes and 40 seconds? Are we to imagine a fusion process that has lungs?[41]

As Temple notes, the solar wind itself is predominantly of positive charge, *except* during these short breathing breaks, where it appears to be "recharging" with a steady stream of electrons in filaments from the galaxy.

In short, the Sun may indeed be a big hot ball of thermonuclear plasma, but the more primary fact is that it is a *plasma*, and *a part of a much larger plasma circuit*.

Two things are worth noting before we continue. The constant stream of positive particles that constitutes the solar wind was noticed and noted by Tesla, who at times noted that the *aether lumeniferous* of 19th century physics was energetic and hydrodynamic. It was Tesla whose impulse electrical experiments may thus said to be, along with the experiments and observations of Norwegian physicist Birkeland, and later of course of Hannes Alfvén, who may be said to be one of the pioneering fathers of plasma physics.

The second thing to note is that the chained-up hydrogen bomb model of the Sun, of a constantly exploding thermonuclear chain reaction constrained by gravity, was the model

[41] Ibid., pp. 125-126.

proposed by the British astrophysicist Sir Arthur Eddington,[42] whom, it will be recalled, played such a pivotal role in fudging the numbers of the 1921 solar eclipse study and verification of General Relativity, and who played such a role in anointing Albert Einstein as the greatest physicist of all time.

But if Einstein won a crown in physics, perhaps it is time to acknowledge that the crown is not that of an emperor or king, but at best probably only the golden or silver circlet of a baronet.[43]

---

[42] Robert Temple, *A New Science of Heaven*, p. 123.

[43] As I was writing this book, I received an email from a member of my website whom we shall simply call "P.T." The email referenced my frequent mentions of Lockheed Skunk Works' late chief Ben Rich's alleged remarks that "we found an error in the equations, and now we can take E.T. home." Of course, this story has made its rounds on the internet and in the UFOlogy community, but no one ever seems to ask *whose* equations and *what* error? P.T. brought to my attention a paper that I had never heard of before, but that is well worth considering as a potential answer to those questions. The paper is titled "Mechanics.—On the Analytic Expressions that Must Be Given to the Gravitational Tensor in Einstein's Theory," (*Rendiconti della Reala Accademia dei* Lincei 26, 381 [1917] authored by none other than one of the "*inventors"* of the tensor analysis, Tullio Levi-Civita (author of the tensor textbook, *The Absolute Differential Calculus* [Dover, 2013, ISBN 978-0-486-63401-2]). It is thus an important paper, the more so since at the very beginning of it, Levi-Civita states—very clearly and unequivocally—that "everything (in Einstein's General Relativity) depends on the incorrect form assumed for the gravitational tensor. We shall see that with our determination any possibility for paradox automatically disappears." The *end* of Levi-Civita's paper is even more breathtaking and worth citing here: "Now it is well known that differential invariants of the 1° order which are intrinsic, like *G**, exclusively formed with the

2. Ball Lightning, Plasma Drones, Intelligence, and Artificial Intelligence

When considering the strange behavior of plasmas as an indicator of possible life, no inventory would be complete without a glance at ball lightning. The Nazis, of course, conducted research into ball lightning prior to and during World War Two in a project codenamed "Charite-Anlage," the name of the hospital in Berlin where the experiments were allegedly conducted. After the war, ball lightning research was conducted in the Soviet Union and the United States,

---

coefficients of ds^2 and with their first derivatives, do *not* exist. **This is enough to render, at least in general, not admissible the form of the gravitational tensor taken by Einstein.** The latter however had already felt some uneasiness, in particular when after having outlined with genial simplicity the theory of gravitational waves, he was led to the unacceptable result that also *spontaneous* waves should as a rule give rise to dispersion of energy through irradiation.

"'Since this fact'—these are his words—'should not happen in nature, it seems likely that quantum theory should intervene by modifying not only Maxwell's electrodynamics, but also the new theory of gravitation.'

"Actually there is no need of reaching to quanta. It is enough to correct the formal expression of the gravitational tensor in the way shown here." (Tullio Levi-Civita, "On the Analytic Expression that Must be given to the Gravitational Tensor in Einstein's Theory," §9, concluding three paragraphs, boldface emphasis added by me.) Of course, by now it is evident that the "gravitational approach" is dealing with the physics of the one percent. Levi-Civitta himself modified his critique after a considerable private correspondence with Einstein, and included an extensive section on relativity in his textbook *The Absolute Differential Calculus*, pp. 354-435. But even here, see his critique of Einstein from p. 438f.

with Russian plasma physicist Piotr Kapitza maintaining that the mysterious phenomenon was an example of plasma physics, and might thus be reproduced and ultimately controllable in the laboratory.[44]

Among the many phenomena that have been associated with ball lightning, UFOs are at the top of the list, and for good reason: the ability of ball lightning to turn on a dime, to accelerate or decelerate suddenly, explain characteristics often associated with UFOs.[45] Ball lightning has been reported

> Inside Second World War American submarines running along the floor; and it has often occurred in airborne planes. It also goes up and down chimneys, and it sometimes appears to 'inspect' things such as patterns on carpets; it can explode, it can be dangerous, and it can even kill people on rare occasions. Usually it is harmless, but sometimes it is deadly.[46]

Yet another recent development in the phenomena of ball lightning must be added to Temple's list, and that is the frequent reports of ball lightning being present during and apparently actually contributing to the formation of crop circles.

In this connection the work of Winston Harper Bostick for the US Atomic Energy Commission must be mentioned.

---

[44] C. Maxwell Cade and Delphine Davis, *The Taming of the Tunderbolts* (London: Abelard-Schuman, 1969, Obsolete Standard Book Number 200-71531-3), p. 14.

[45] Much of Cade's and Davis's book is a compilation of eyewitness reports dealing with ball lightning and its strange properties, and a whole chapter is devoted to the subject of "Fireballs and Flying Saucers." See Cade and Davis, *The Taming of the Thunderbolts*, pp. 105-118.

[46] Robert Temple, *A New Science of Heaven*, p. 51.

Bostick actually invented a kind of "plasma cannon" that fired "plasmoids" as he called them; these consisted of a torus- or doughnut-like structure. He quickly learned that these would and could move clean through solid objects like ball lightning was reported to do.[47] Moreover, when two to four plasmoids were fired at each other, the result was astonishing: they appeared to form spiraling structures remarkably similar to galaxies, and Bostick drew the obvious conclusion: perhaps galaxies themselves were the result of a similar process of self-organization. The phenomenon, as Temple notes, compelled Bostick to join the growing list of scientists who noticed the resemblance of plasma to life on account of its ability to self-organize and to preserve itself.[48]

---

[47] Robert Temple, *A New Science of Heaven*, pp. 140-142.

[48] Ibid., pp. 144. Cade and Davis refer to these efforts to produce plasmas by a plasma gun in the following way in their book: "A study of magnetically confined plasmas was made at the University of California Radiation Laboratory about eight years ago… A plasma gun was constructed which generated a plasma of deuterium. Two electrodes made of titanium with absorbed deuterium were used to strike an arc of several thousand amperes, with a pulse duration of about half a microsecond. The intensity of the arc evaporated electrons and ions from the two electrodes, and the magnetic field associated with the current-pulse pinched the plasma into a slender column. The doughnut-shaped plasmoids were magnetically expelled from the gun with a velocity of about 120 miles per second. Although the plasmoids moved at such tremendous speed, they left a luminous wake which could be recorded with a high speed camera. Although seemingly unrelated, this work was a vital link in the chain of research projects which may eventually lead to the systematic production of artificial lightning balls. One apparatus for making small spherical plasmoids has been developed by the Bendix Research Laboratoroes; another, developed in the U.S.S.R., is stated to use a quartz tube with a special profile, and with a core of refractory

Bostick went on to propose that the Sun's solar wind actually consisted of such plasmoids, an idea that was "later adopted by Hannes Alfvén" who viewed the Sun as a gigantic plasma gun firing the plasmoids.[49] Within the plasma life hypothesis, however, Robert Temple elaborates another possibility about plasmoids, one which also rationalizes the odd behavior reported in connection to some ball lightning rather well:

> What is important for our argument here is that giant plasmoids from the Sun, given the complex behavior that led Bostick to think of them as living enttites, could easily be so intricate and complex in their structure that… they could even be intelligent or conscious entities. The implications of that would be truly limitless. Just imagine, for instance, that every plasmoid belched forth by the Sun and reaching the Earth or one of the Kordylewski clouds could be in effect a program (in the sense of a computer program) and in that sense a communication of intelligence.[50]

---

material which carries electric arcs." (Cade and Davis, *The Taming of the Thunderbolts*, p. 145). It should be noted that the apparatus as described also bears a strong resemblance to the huge underground quartz lens and electrical arc facility discovered after World War Two at the University of Heidelberg in Germany. Given the heavy investment the Nazis made in plasma research from the Bell project, to the alleged ball lightning project called Charite-Anlage, to the post-war research on fusion and the claims made for plasma by Nazi-Argentinian physicist Ronald Richter, it is safe to say that the Heidelberg facility probably was a component in what appears to be a vast Nazi project in the control and manipulation of plasma. Q.v. my *Reich of the Black Sun* (Kempton, Illinois: Adventures Unlimited Press, 2004), pp. 221-222, 225-226.

[49] Robert Temple, *A New Science of Heaven*, p. 150.

[50] Ibid., p. 151.

In other words, plasmoids and ball lightning might be types of "plasma drones," projections of an "intelligent plasma" designed to probe or reconnoiter an area. Temple notes that the acoustic "noisiness" of the double layers in plasmas might account for the strange signals that Bostick detected in this laboratory experiments, signals that he qualified as structurally "too complex for analysis."[51]

3. Leidenfrost Layers, Ambiplasmas, or Plasmas with Regions of Matter and Antimatter

In addition to double layers and the resulting abilities of plasmas to maintain discrete regions of differing charge or temperatures, these abilities also allow the resolution of a yet another problem that has dogged cosmological physics: the matter-antimatter problem. Alfvén puts it this way:

> Is it possible for matter and antimatter to co-exist in the universe? If so, could they co-exist even within our galaxy?
>
> *As long as all astrophysical models were basically homogeneous, the answer had to be negative. The modern views according to which plasmas usually are inhomongeneous and especially the discovery of the cellular structure of space has changed the situation.*
>
> (Matter-antimatter) annihilation seems to be the only reasonable source of energy for a number of extremely energetic phenomena, such as the Hubble Expansion…and a number of other phenomena which are now being explored by X-ray and γ-ray astronomers.[52]

---

[51] Robert Temple, *A New Science of Heaven*, p. 151.

[52] Hannes Alfvén, *Cosmic Plasma*, p. 102, emphasis added. Alfvén coins the term "ambiplasma" for plamsas consisting of interior regions of matter and antimatter (q.v. p. 98).

While Alfvén does not rule out the possibility that ordinary "double layers" might separate such regions of ambiplasma—in this case layers of electrons and positrons (an antimatter electron with positive, rather than negative, charge)—he also hypothesizes that such separation membranes might actually be Leidenfrost layers. A Leidenfrost layer is a layer of hot vapor or gas that actually insulates the rest of a compound from intense heat. For example, if one drops some water into a pan that has been heated to extraordinary temperature, a Leifenfrost layer of water vapor forms between the pan and the rest of the water which actually insulates that water, and keeps it from boiling away.[53]

The significance of this hypothesis may be missed until one recalls two factors: (1) the cosmic extent of plasmas themselves, and (2) the internal cellular structure of plasmas that sheaths and double layers permit. Add Leidenfrost layers to this, and one not only obtains a cellular structure to space, but also a structure which may in turn consist of ambiplasma which, through annihilation reactions, would be of sufficient energy perhaps to account for the expansion of the universe that is observed.[54]

Cosmic plasmas, in other words, not only *are* that "dark matter" and "dark energy" of modern theory, they are *not*, unlike those concepts, mere mathematical artifacts; they would also appear to be the actual basis for the 19th century's theory of a super-fine matter pervading all space (and more dense matter!) called the *aether lumeniferous*, or even older mediaeval and classical notions of the universe as an organism rather than mechanism, and of space as a crystal.

---

[53] Hannes Alfvén, *Cosmic Plasma*, p. 104.

[54] Q.v. Alfvén, *Cosmic Plasma*, and the discussion on pp. 138-139.

4. When Plasmas Intersect with Plasmas: Bioplasma Bodies, Biophotons, Kirlian Photography, and the Astral or Spiritual Body

Robert Temple in his book *A New Science of Heaven* records the result of a curious experiment conducted at Northwestern University in the U.S.A. In the experiment, small polystyrene plastic spheres or beads were placed in oil and left alone, to wander in the small currents of the oil. Then, an electric field was pulsed, and the small plastic beads began doing a remarkable thing: they began to spin and, moreover, to gather in roiling clusters "which resembled the swarming of bacteria."[55] Temple notes that: "At a fundamental level, we see here with the lifelike behavior of inanimate particles so precisely mimicking living things that even the very definition of 'life' is threatened."[56] But perhaps it is not the definition or understanding of *life* that is threatened; after all, we saw with our cursory examination of St. John of Damascus that his understanding of "life" was considerably broader and deeper than the "modern" view, and the hypothesis of plasma life can be viewed as a return to an older view. It is thus not so much the understanding of *life* that is threatened, but the understanding of *nonlife* that has changed.

In any case, once one arrives at the idea that cosmic plasmas or plasmas in general might be the basis of older views such as an ultra-fine matter or *aether lumeniferous* that pervades all space and more dense matter, other implications immediately follow. For example, it becomes possible to posit, as did the Soviet plasma physicist Kamenetsky, that plasmas may exist "within living organisms,"[57] and if plasmas

[55] Robert Temple, *A New Science of Heaven*, p. 24.

[56] Ibid.

[57] Ibid., p. 20.

are indeed living inorganic life forms, then one life form exists inside another, without either losing their individuality or distinctiveness. Again, the cellular structure of plasmas also suggested to Japanese physicist Hiroyuki Ikezi that plasmas were a special form of crystal, which could in turn store and retrieve information, and thus function as a basis of intelligence.[58] Once one arrived at this point, then it was possible that since crystals emitted photons under stress—the piezoelectric effect—that DNA, as an aperiodic crystal of its own, and a helical structure resembling that of the current helixes formed in a plasma pinch, it became possible to envision a "bioenergetics" and even the idea that organic life emits "biophotons"—a very faint glow given off by all living things—that can be and actually has been detected and photographed. These biophotons along with the bacteria cloud that exists around living things form a bioenergetics endothermic cloud of plasma, in this case, a plasma of both organic and non-organic regions![59] Viewed in this way, the less dense "plasma" body does not appear to exist inside the more dense material body, but the reverse, the more dense body appears to exist inside the less dense one, or to put it more succinctly and with more force: we are *not* "souls imprisoned in a body," but rather a body inside a soul.

---

[58] Robert Temple, *A New Science of Heaven*, pp. 21-22.

[59] Ibid., pp. 180, 215, 238-239, 247, 267. Temple hypothesizes that the so-called "life" and "death" flashes are biophoton phenomena, a hypothesis with obvious implications for one of the world's oldest and most revered relics, the Shroud of Turin. In the case of the Shroud, if it is a biophotonic event recorded on the cloth, then it is one magnitudes of order more powerful than ordinary biophotons. Temple also hypothesizes that such biophotonic plasmas also are the basis for the idea of an "astral" or "spiritual" body, connected with the Kirlian photography discovered in the Soviet Union.

If crystals store photons, and DNA (and plasmas!) are aperiodic crystals, and if photons are the means of quantum entanglement and the memory and communication of specific information over vast distances, then it would appear that yet another function of plasmas is as "entanglement machines," able to self-organize—like the Sloan Great wall—over truly vast and cosmic distances of space and time.

E. Conclusions: A Summary of Characteristics of Plasmas Paralleling those of Intelligent Life

When one compiles all this together, one ends with an inventory of plasmas that, according to Temple, are remarkably similar to those associated not only with life, but with intelligent life:

> Plasmas are bounded entities that persist through time, a characteristic of any living organism at the most basic level.
>
> Plasmas may feed on fresh plasma, and be nourished, for example, by solar winds. They may even compete for such food. Plasmoids seem to bond with one another and interact in other ways.
>
> We have seen particles in plasmas swarming like microbial beings… and forming other patterns such as hexagonal structures, spirals, concentric circles and double-helix patterns… Nerve-like filaments grow in plasmas, including those that form double helixes and may carry information as well as energy. Plasmas seethe with movement in and around their own internal structures created by electromagnetic fields. Complex plasma entities have countless plasmoid regions within them, all protected within their sheaths and separated by 'voids', like organs in animal bodies.
>
> …

> We have seen… that the crystalline structure of complex dusty plasmas makes them potentially far more complex than human bodies. There are soft, broadly crystal-like structures that grow into beautiful and intricate entities with the ability to transmit information over vast distances. Particles within a plasma can interact in concert with other particles.
>
> Furthermore… the mysterious ability to move through objects without changing form, seen in quantum mechanics in phenomena associated with solitons and sometimes called 'tunnelling' takes places between 'organs' in a plasma….
>
> There is no universally agreed, mathematically precise set of defining qualities of a living entity, but most accounts include growth, cellular form, reproduction, response to stimuli, ability to perceive and process energy.
>
> … Vadim Nikolaevich Tsytovich wrote in 2007 that the principles used to define life are:
>
> autonomy
> evolution
> autopoieis (a system capable of reproducing and maintaining itself)
>
> He concluded that:
>
> *Complex organized plasma structures exhibit all the necessary properties to qualify them as candidates for inorganic living matter that may exist in space provided certain conditions allow them to evolve naturally.*[60]

From such considerations as these it becomes rather obvious that those warning of the dangers that artificial intelligence networks might "transduce" higher dimensional entities and intelligences—Elon Musk for example—are not indulging in

[60] Robert Temple, *A New Science of Heaven*, pp. 163-165, emphasis added.

mere idle speculation. Such networks are by nature, like plasmas, electromagnetic in nature.

Temple is also alive to this type of possibility, and to the vast power that such "ancient and bodiless powers" (to give them their standard Christian designation) would have:

> Intelligent calculations by such conscious plasmas would be so rapid and so massive that a Kordylewski Cloud would easily have the capacity to monitor every living creature on Earth in real time and model future events for all of them. Such a cloud could thus foresee with a high degree of probability what would happen in almost any Earth situation, and have models of every conceivable variable's effect on events. From the point of view of the limited human brain, a kordylewski Cloud therefore has the capacity of what to us would be indistinguishable from omniscience.[61]

Sometimes, however, an argument is best advanced not by scientists and equations nor even by thinkers of broad curiosity and deep learning such as Robert Temple.

Sometimes a few pictures can be worth a thousand words, as the old Chinese aphorism has it. In this case, a few pictures is the best way of summarizing and illustrating the argument...

---

[61] Robert Temple, *A New Science of Heaven*, p. 227.

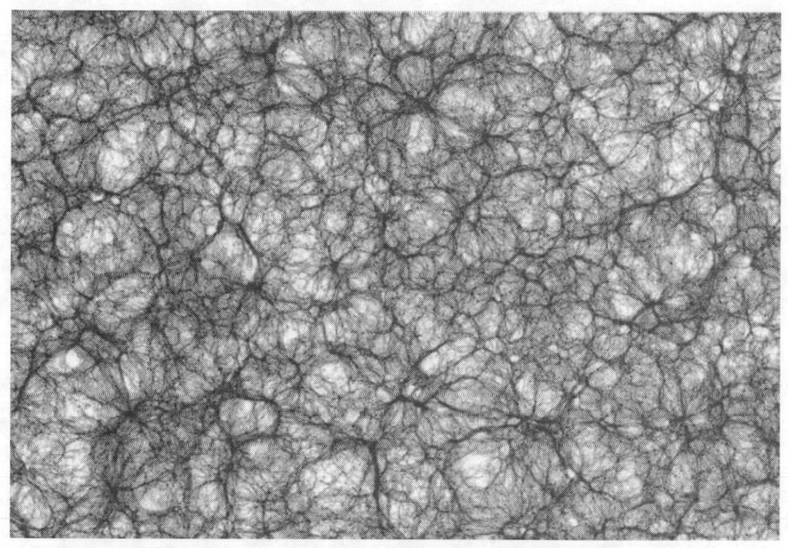

The "Cosmic Web" in Negative View: Cosmic Plasma filaments

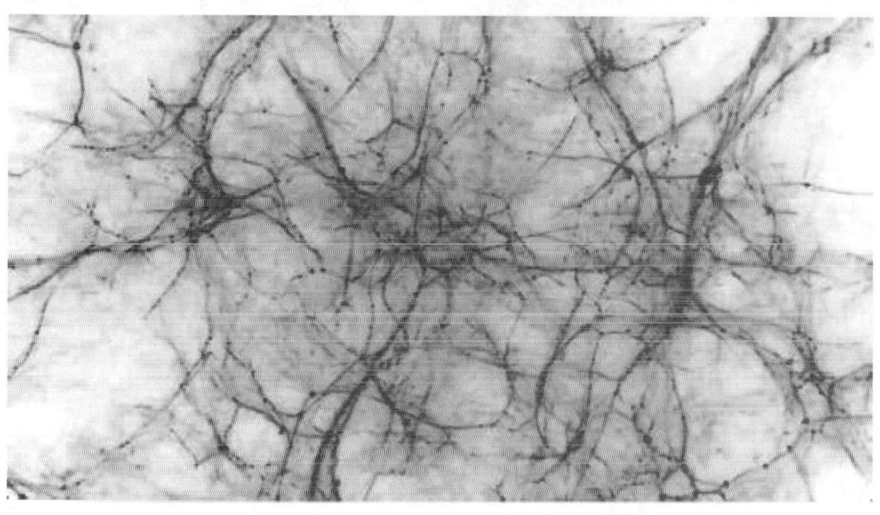

Another negative view of the "Cosmic Web" of plasma filaments filling galactic and inter-galactic space

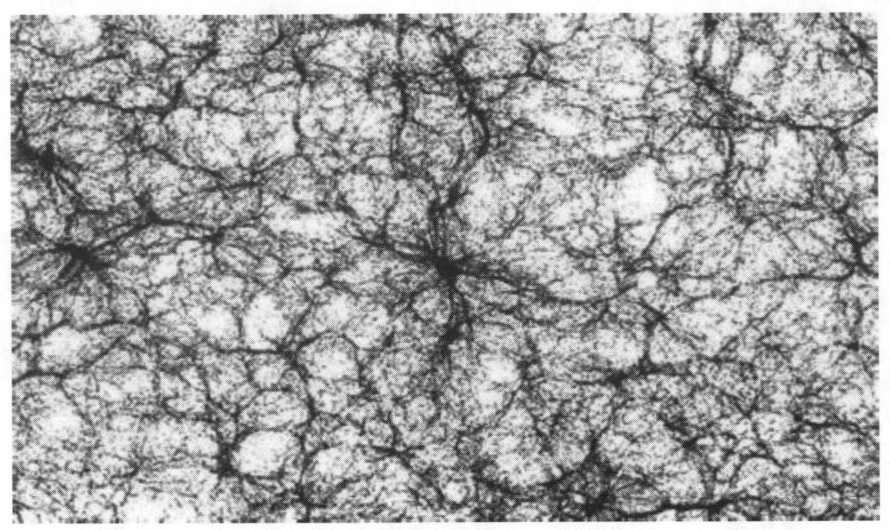

Yet another negative view of the "Cosmic Web" of plasma filaments filling galactic and intergalactic space

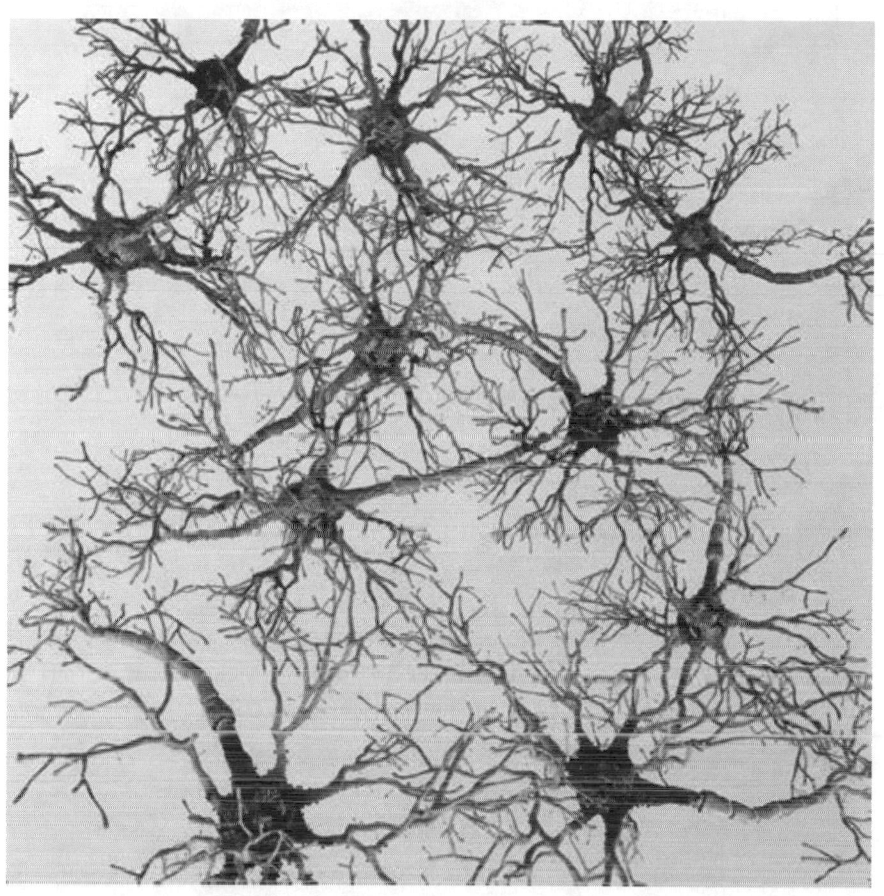

Negative View of the Neurons of a Human Brain

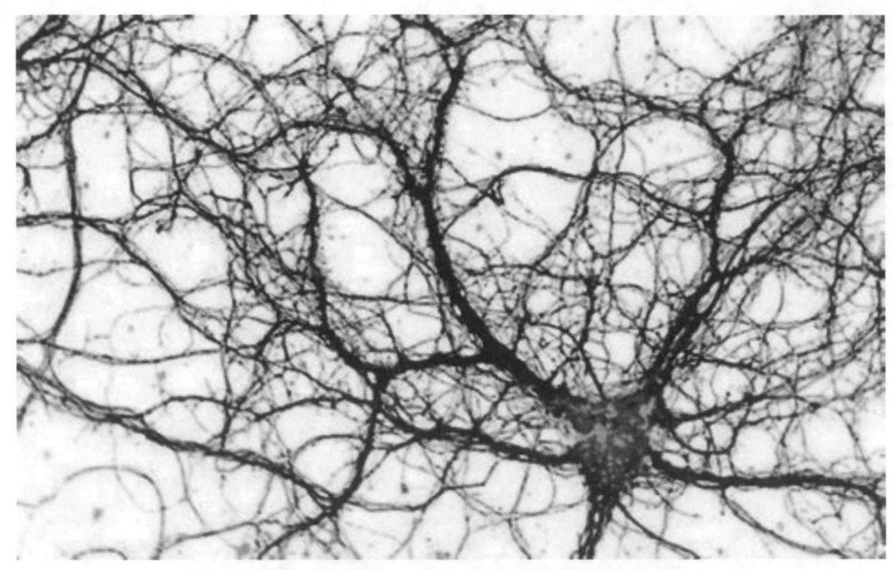

Negative View of the Neurons of a Brain

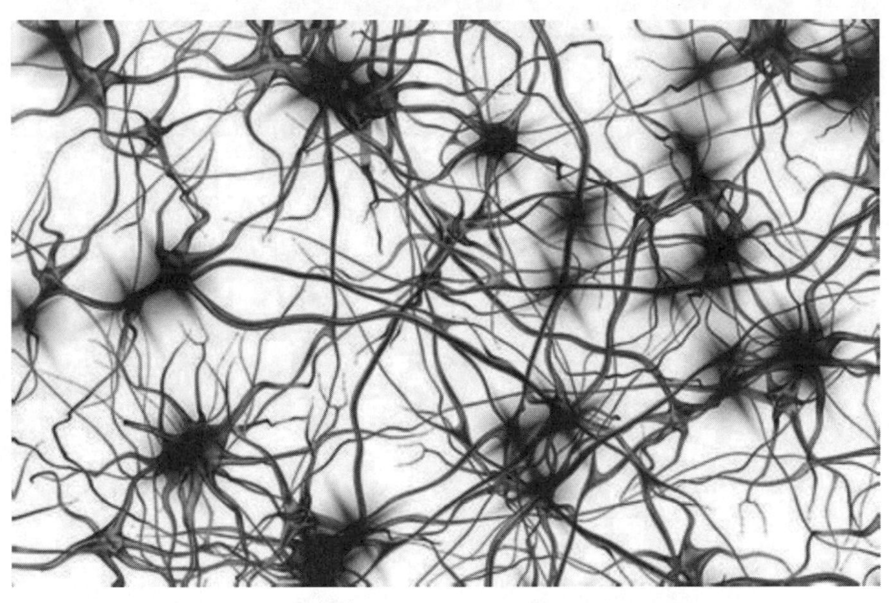

Negative view of Neurons in a brain

4
THE DEMON IN THE *EKUR* AND THE GREAT PYRAMID WEAPON HYPOTHESIS:
THE EXPLANATORY POWER OF THE PLASMA LIFE HYPOTHESIS

"But obviously, our present actions cannot determine the past. *The past is the 'unchangeable truth of history.' Or is it?"*
Physicists Bruce Rosenblum and Fred Kuttner[1]

"We have reversed the usual classical notion that the independent 'elementary parts' of the world are the fundamental reality, and that the various systems are merely particular contingent forms and arrangements of these parts. Rather, ***we say that inseparable quantum interconnectedness of the whole universe is the fundamental reality,*** *and that relatively independently behaving parts are merely the particular and contingent forms within this whole."*
Physicist David Bohm[2]

ONCE ONE TAKES THE GREAT PYRAMID Weapon Hypothesis seriously, and stirs that in with the Plasma Life Hypothesis, and then kneads it all together with the Damascene's observations on angels and demons, and garnishes the whole result with Sitchin's epigraph about demons dwelling in the artificial "mountains" that are "over

---

[1] Cited in Mark Gober, *An End to Upside Down Thinking: Dispelling the Myth that the Brain Produces Consciousness, and the Implications for Everyday Life* (Cardiff-by-the-Sea, California: Waterside Press, ISBN 978-947637-85-6), p. 43.

[2] D.J. Bohm, and B.J. Hiley, "On the Intuitive Understanding of Nonlocality as Implied by Quantum Theory." *Foundations of Physics 5,* No. 1 (1975): 93-109, cited in Gober, *An End to Upside Down Thinking*, p. 48, emphasis added by Gober.

the horizon," i.e., in Egypt, then the result is a profound modification of the Weapon Hypothesis, one which, moreover, rationalizes a great many other things in one fell swoop. As will hopefully become clear in this chapter, the Weapon Hypothesis does *not* require the Plasma Life Hypothesis nor Sitchin's "Demon in the *Ekur*." But once one admits both, that hypothesis is profoundly modified both in a variety of direct ways and in wider and more peripheral implications.

A. Friends (or Enemies) in High Places

But exactly what are some of those peripheral implications? For instance, in the study of comparative religion it is not long before one encounters whole *patterns* of associations of gods and demons with various types of places. The work of Romanian religion scholar Mircea Eleade is full of references to sacred grottos, caves, valleys, rivers, lakes, and, of course, mountains. One need not think long nor hard to recall more popular and well-known versions of this specific association: Zeus and the Greek gods dwelling on Mount Olympus, Moses meeting Yahweh on Mount Sinai, and throughout many books of the Old Testament, the association of the *Ba'alim*, the Baals of idolatry, with the "high places" used for their worship.

With "Sitchin's epigraph," however, we are confronted by something much more direct, and much more primal. Let us remind ourselves one more time what he said: "An Akkadian 'Book of Job' titled *Ludlul Bel Nimeqi ("I praise the Lord of Deepness")* refers to the 'irresistable demon that has exited from the *Ekur'* in a land 'across the horison, in the lower World (Africa).'"[3] Recall from the second chapter of this book that Sitchin also argued that such early Sumerian texts

[3] Zecharia Sitchin, *The Wars of Gods and Men*, p. 140.

and legends should be interpreted with reference to the Giza compound, and the Great Pyramid in particular, precisely because the *ekurs* depicted in Sumerian art were *not* the stepped pyramid-zigurrats of Mesopotamia, but the *smooth-sided* pyramids that are typical of Egypt.

As I pointed previously in this book in chapter two, Sumerian depictions of pyramids are almost uniformly that of smooth-sided structures, and *not* the stepped pyramids common to Mesopotamian zigurrats, and for this reason Sitchin concluded that some Mesopotamian texts should be read as references to the pyramids of Giza, let us refresh our memory on what these depictions looked like:

Early Sumerican Depiction of a Smooth-Sided Pyramid

Early Sumerian Depiction of a Smooth-Sided Pyramid

Another Sumerian Depiction of a Smooth-Sided Pyramid with Wings

Early Sumerian Depiction of a Smooth-Sided Pyramid with "horizontal cadducues" and double-counter-rotating Ouroboros

Now let us extend our observations of the implications of Sumerian depictions by looking closely at the cuneiogram of ekur" itself:

Composite Akkadian Cuneiogram for "Ekur," Pyramid, Mountain, Mountain-House;

This cuneiogram can mean or be translated as "mountain" and is used to refer to pyramids or zigurrats, but it can also mean a "mountain house," i.e., a special pyramidal dwelling of the gods and demons. In this case, the *ekur* is synonymous with yet another term that can be used for a pyramid: a *Dur-An-Ki*, a "bond*(Dur)*-heaven(*An*)-Ki(*earthi)*."

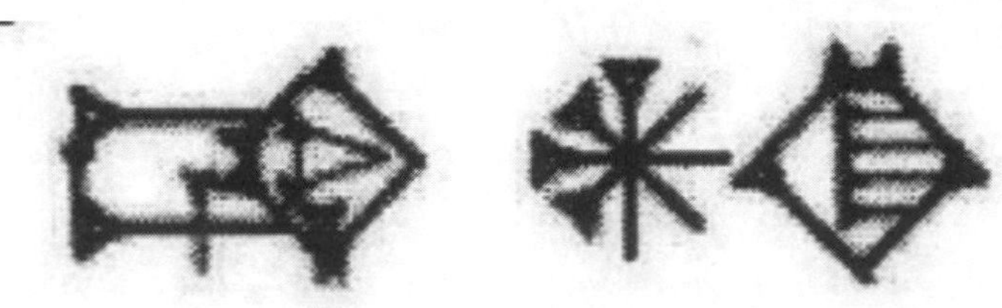

Composite Akkadian Cuneiogram of (from left to right)
Dur-An-Ki:
Bond-Heaven-Earth

Certainly the type of physics I have speculated underlying the Great Pyramid is a physics that literally links the heavens to the Earth, and thus the name *Dur-An-Ki* for a pyramid makes sense from the Weapon Hypothesis point of view.

However, while Sitchin never mentions it in connection with his "Demon-in-the-*Ekur*" epigram, he might have pointed out that the cuneiogram for *Ekur*" is a *composite*, consisting of the rectangular element on the left side for "house," and the *three wedges* representing "mountains" on the right, almost as if the cuneiogram is making deliberate reference to the Giza Compound and its three large, smooth-sided pyramids as a literal "Mountain House" or dwelling place of a demon. Thus, with *ekur* as the "mountain house" of a demon dwelling at Giza and as the focus of his "Pyramid

Wars" of gods and men, Sitchin has provided a rationale for why pyramids have been associated with such grizzly and unabashedly demonic activity such as human sacrifice.

B. An Extreme Speculation Concerning Giza, The "Demon in the Ekur," and the Governance of the World

With these Sumerian depictions of smooth-sided pyramids and our brief excursion into Akkadian cuneiograms in hand, we may now consider another of the wider peripheral implications of the "Demon in the Ekur," namely, these two well-known diagrams of the location of Giza from Piazzi-Smyth, the famous 19th century Astronomer Royal of Scotland and advocate of the Pyramid-as-Prophecy:

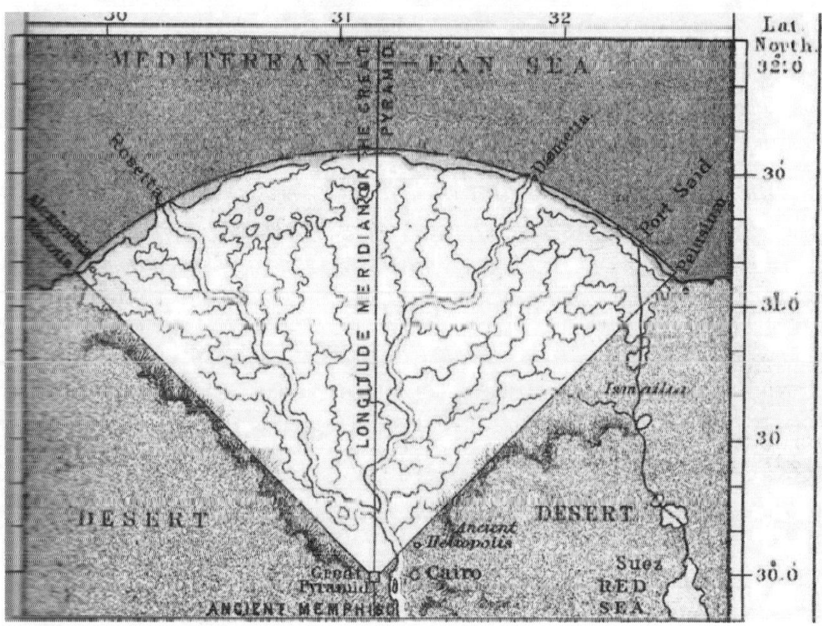

Piazzi-Smyth's diagram of the location of Giza on the axis of symmetry of the Nile Delta[4]

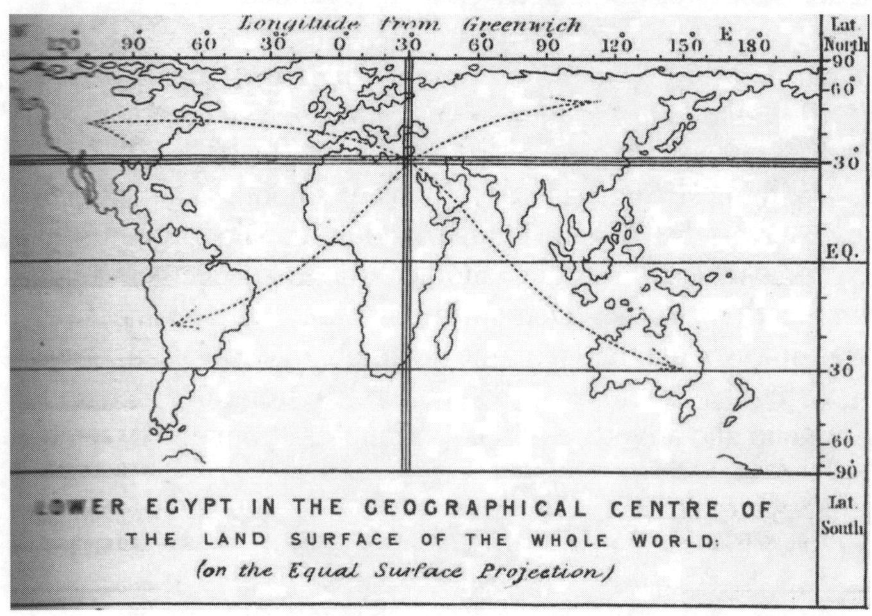

Piazzi-Smyth's diagram of Giza as the Prime Meridian, located at the center of the surface land mass of the Earth[5]

From the standpoint of the Weapon Hypothesis as elaborated in my book *The Giza Death Star Revisited*, the location of the Great Pyramid as a coupled harmonic oscillator of the planet, and of local space, makes abundant sense, for the selection of the site in the center of the planetary surface land mass can be

---

[4] Charles Piazzi-Smyth, F.R.S.E., F.R.A.S, *The Great Pyramid: Its Secrets and Mysteries Revealed* (New York: Bell Publishing Company, No date, reprint of the 1880 edition of *Our Inheritance in the Great Pyramid*, ISBN 0-517-26403-X), inset, plate II.

[5] Ibid.

rationalized on the basis of making the oscillator as efficient as possible over that surface.

But the plasma-life hypothesis coupled with that of the "Demon in the *Ekur"* means that the selection of the site may also have involved other motivations. As I detailed in my book *Grid of the Gods*, the megalithic metrologist Carl Munck worked out the elaborate mathematics behind the positioning of several of this planet's megalithic structures and their locations, and all of them appear to have been worked out on the basis of Giza's Great Pyramid's apex being the longitude of an ancient prime meridian.[6]

As we saw in chapter two in our brief examination of St. John of Damascus' review of angelology, it is a component of the lore of angels and demons that specific planets, and even regions of planets, can have their own "guardian angels," and that the planet Earth's guardian angel actually *rebelled and fell*, leading his own host—and presumably the planet over which he (or she) ruled—into that rebellion.[7] *From the standpoint of selecting a location for a seat of government of the planet by such an entity, the location of Giza at the center of the Earth's surface land mass once again makes perfect sense, especially if the Pyramid itself is the weapon by which that governance is enforced.* One need only reflect on the curious fact that this same understanding of pyramids as seats of cosmological *and* local order and governance also finds its way into the Mesoamerican pyramid cultures, to realize that "Sitchin's epigraph" is not a one-off nor contrary to the overall pattern. *On the contrary, it may rather be the ultimate **basis** and **origin** of the pattern.*

---

[6] Q.v. my *Grid of the Gods: The Aftermath of the Cosmic War and the Physics of the Pyramid Peoples.*

[7] It will be recalled that the text of the *Ludlul Bel Nimeqi* actually refers to Sitchin's "demon in the *ekur*" as a "she-devil."

C. Aspects of the Weapon Hypothesis Modified by the Plasma Life Hypothesis

With this in mind, we may now dive more deeply into the specifics of the Weapon Hypothesis as elaborated in my previous Great Pyramid books, and in *The Cosmic War,* in order to see how the hypothesis of intelligent plasma life and "a demon in the *ekur*" modifies those specifics, in this case, the hypothesized metamaterial crystals in the structure, and the overall nature of the structure itself as a crystal, "coil," and waveguide.[8] As we will now see, the Plasma Life Hypothesis ties together a number of areas that previously only seemed distantly related to each other.

1. Crystals: Tuners and Transducers
a. The Planetary Associations of Angels: Their Occult Sigils and Seals, "Circuits," and Crop Circles

In my very first foray into the field of alternative research, *The Giza Death Star*, I had to do several things at once, in addition to outlining a speculative case that the Great Pyramid was a weapon. As I indicated in *The Giza Death Star Revisited,*[9] one of the things I was attempting to do was to make a wider case for analogical thinking in general, and how it formed such an important part of ancient cosmology and methods of thought. As a result, the argument for the Weapon Hypothesis itself suffered for a lack of clarity and concision.

One such area of "analogical thinking" that I covered in *The Giza Death Star* is now worth mentioning here in the context of the intelligent plasma life hypothesis, for the context for such thinking has become—no pun intended—

---

[8] For the discussion of these crystals in conjunction with the Weapon Hypothesis, see my *Giza Death Star Revisited.*

[9] See the introduction to my *Giza Death Star Revisited.*

crystal clear. That area is the strong resemblance of some occult sigils and seals of the planets, and the seals of their guardian angels or bodiless intelligences with *the schematics of electrical circuit components*, and the wider resemblance of such seals with crystalline structures.[10] Some well-known examples from Manly P. Hall's *Secret Teachings of All Ages* will clarify the point (and note, I have considerably enlarged these drawings from the original in order to render the features of interest clearly):

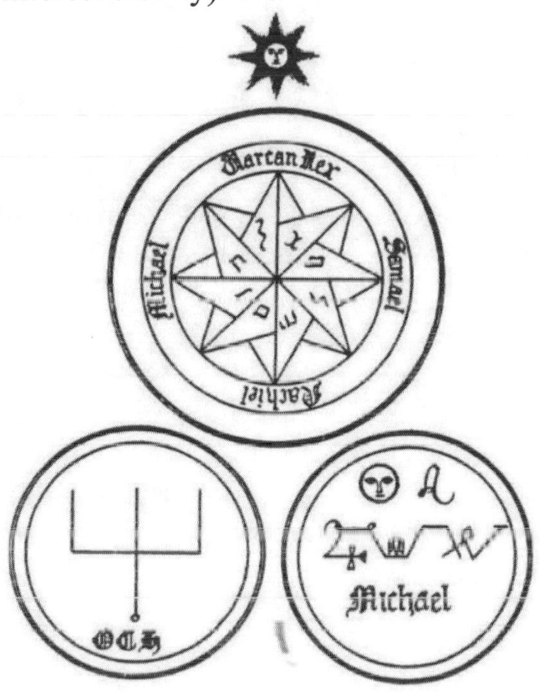

Planetary and Angelic Seal of the Sun[11]

[10] See my *The Giza Death Star* (Kempton, Illinois: Adventures Unlimited Press, 2001), pp. 29-30, and the Corvisss Press reprint of that book on Lulu.com, pp. 29-30.

[11] Manley P. Hall, *The Secret Teachings of All Ages: Masonic, Hermetic, Qabbalistic & Rosicrucian Symbolical*

Planetary and Angelic Seal of Mercury[12]

Philosophy, Being an Interpretation of the Secret Teachings Concealed within the Rituals, Allegories and Mysteries of all Ages (Los Angeles, California: The Philosophical Research Society, Inc., Diamond Jubilee Edition Reduced Facsimile. 1988. ISBN 978-0-89314-548-4), p. civ.

[12] Manly P. Hall, *Secret Teachings of All Ages*, Diamond Jubliee Facsimile Reprint Edition, p. civ.

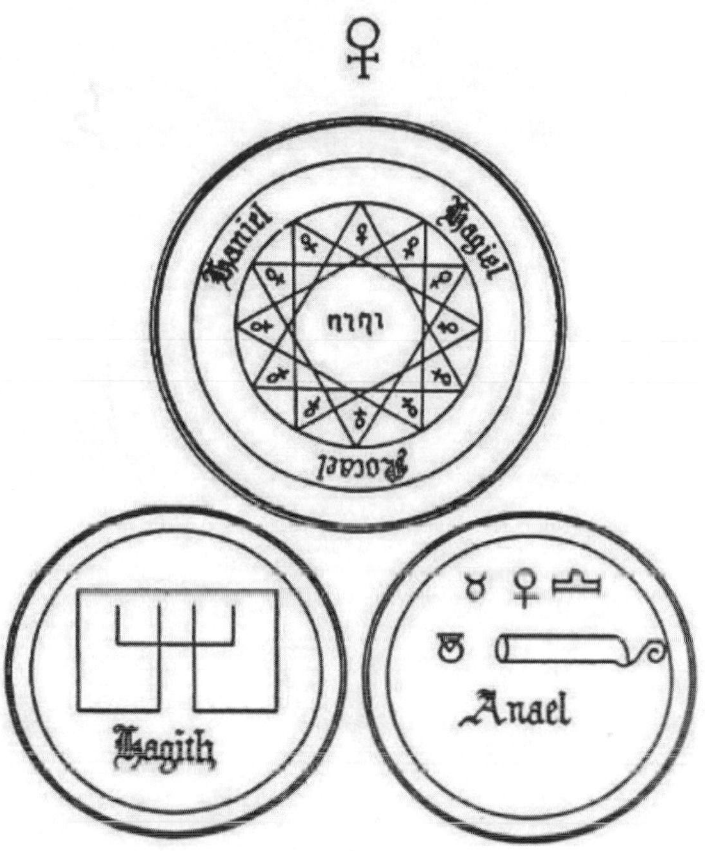

Planetary and Angelic Seal of Venus[13]

---

[13] Manly P. Hall, *Secret Teachings of All Ages*, Diamond Jubliee Facsimile Reprint Edition, p. civ.

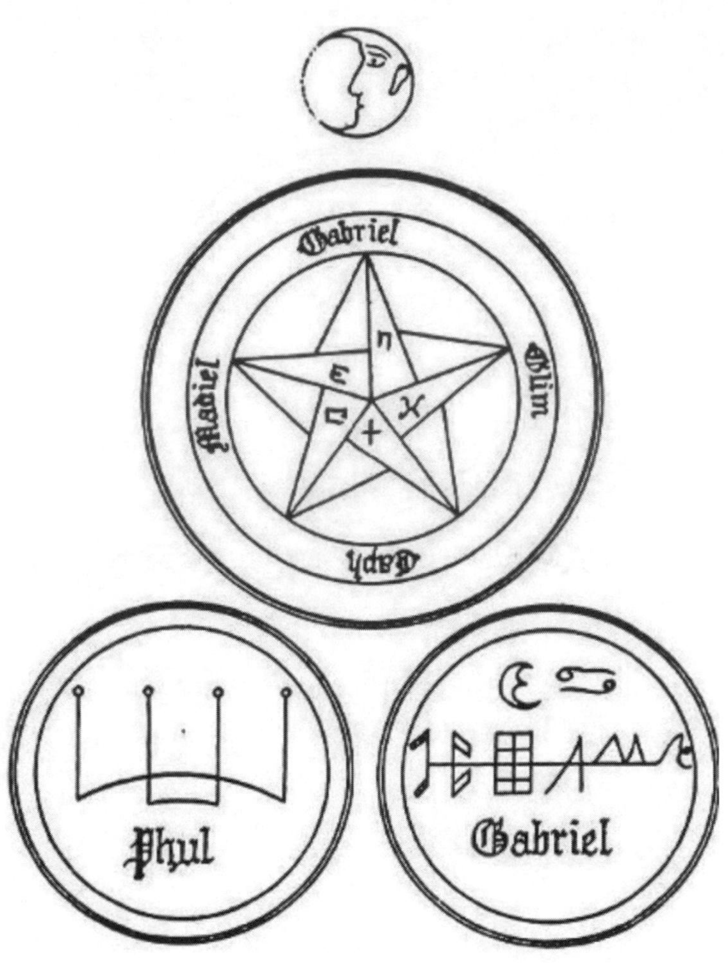

Planetary and Angelic Seals of the Moon[14]

[14] Manly P. Hall, *Secret Teachings of All Ages*, Diamond Jubliee Facsimile Reprint Edition, p. civ.

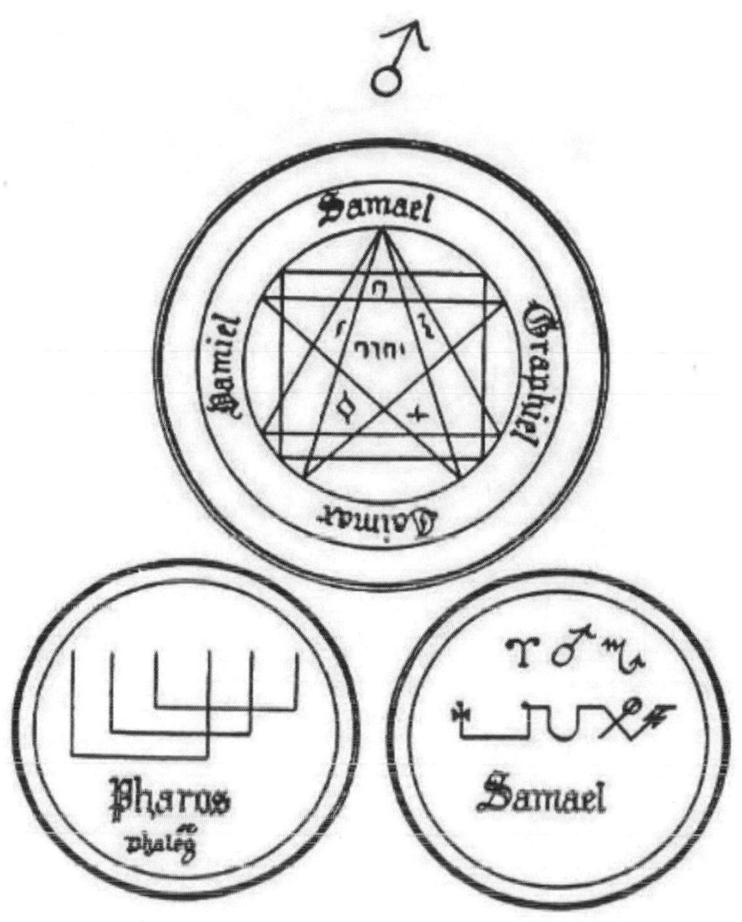

Planetary and Angelic Seals of Mars[15]

[15] Manly P. Hall, *Secret Teachings of All Ages*, Diamond Jubliee Facsimile Reprint Edition, p. civ.

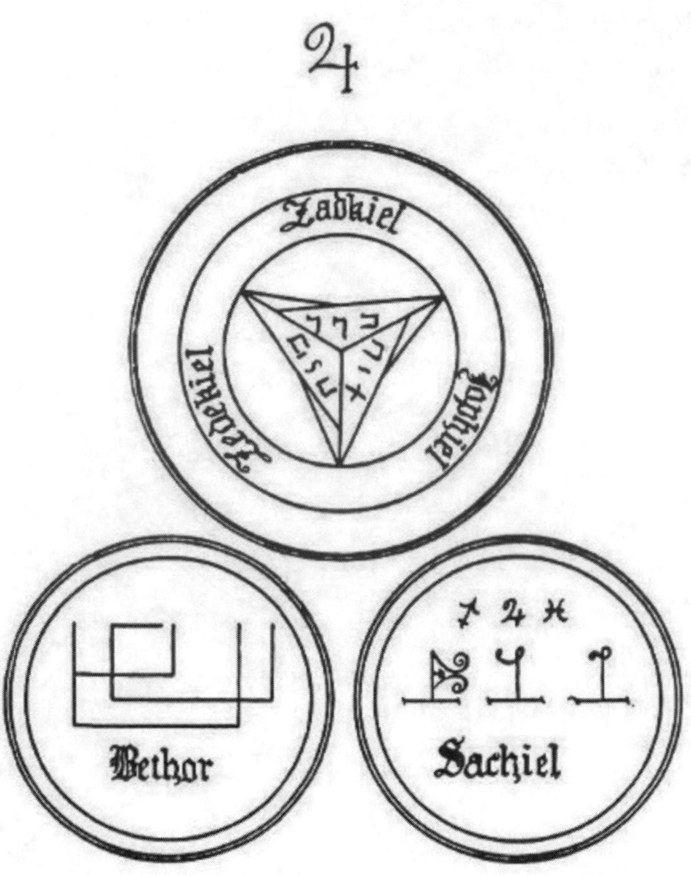

Planetary and Angelic Seals of Jupiter[16]

[16] Manly P. Hall, *Secret Teachings of All Ages*, Diamond Jubliee Facsimile Reprint Edition, p. civ.

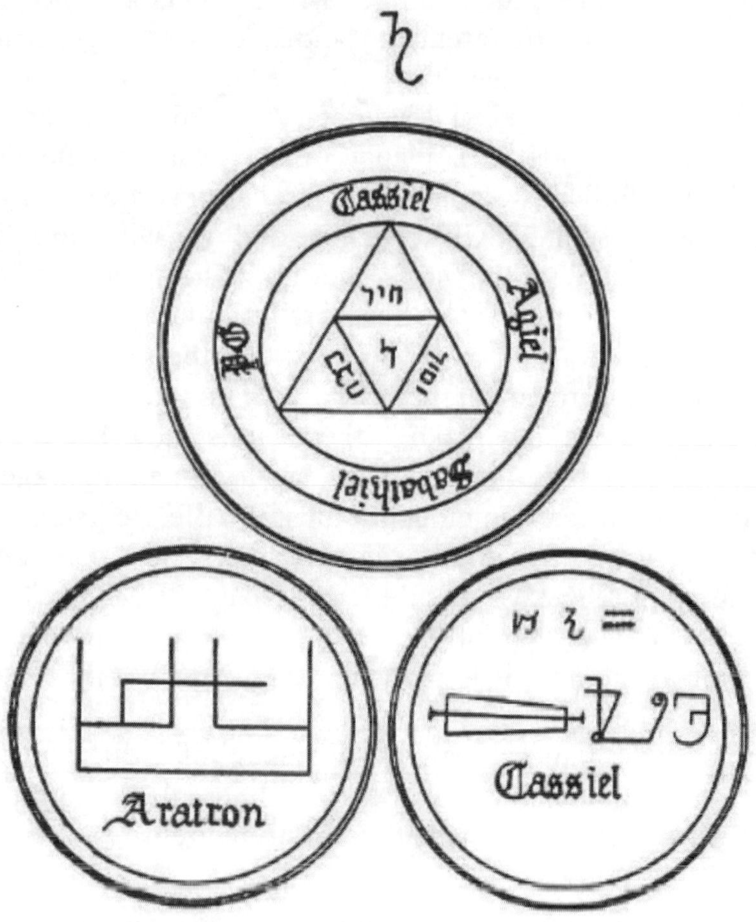

Planetary and Angelic Seals of Saturn[17]

Note that the lower left seal in each case bears strong qualitative resemblances to electrical circuit schematics, including in one or two instances similarities to the symbols for antennae. Note also that the four principal archangels of

[17] Manly P. Hall, *Secret Teachings of All Ages*, Diamond Jubliee Facsimile Reprint Edition, p. civ.

Hebrew scripture and tradition—Michael, Gabriel, Raphael, and Uriel—are represented, and perhaps significantly, Michael, the Archangel that led the angelic hosts against Lucifer, is the Angel and Planetary Guardian of the Sun, which was considered a planet in classical and mediaeval astrology. Similarly, Samael, a name that in some apocryphal literature is associated with rebellion and war with God, is the angel associated with Mars, the god and planet of war. Perhaps most significantly, Earth, with its fallen guardian, is not represented at all, as if to imply that the practitioners of symbolic and ceremonial magic did not "go there."

Whatever one may make of these sigils and seals, they are perhaps themselves a legacy of a long-forgotten high age and civilization where intelligent plasma life, crystals, and electricity were all viewed as deeply interrelated components in one comprehensive picture. In the case of Michael being the angelic guardian of the Sun, the association becomes difficult to ignore. It is perhaps also worth noting that ball lightning-like phenomena have also been seen to be associated with such "seals" and "sigils" of a different type: with the mathematical and "crystalline" designs and the suggestive "circuitry schematics" of crop circles.

b. The Planetary Associations of Crystals with Angels: The Hebrew High Priest's Breastplate and the Gemstones in the Crown of Global Governance

Another of those "peripheral areas" where the intelligent plasma life hypothesis shows an ability to unify seemingly discrete and disconnected areas of esoteric lore is in the association of specific gemstone crystals with certain planets. In my book *The Cosmic War* I cited the following passage from well-known British Egyptologist Wallace-Budge:

> The old astrologers believed that precious and semi-precious stones were bearers of the influences of the Seven Astrological Stars or Planets. Thus they associated with the-
>
> SUN, yellowish or gold-coloured stones, e.g. amber, hyacinth, topaz, chrysolite;
>
> With the MOON, whitish stones, e.g., the diamond, crystal, opal, beryl, mother-of-pearl.
>
> With MARS, red stones, e.g. ruby, haematite, jasper, blood-stone.
>
> With MERCURY, stones of neutral tints, e.g. agate, carnelian, chalcedony, sardonyx.
>
> With JUPITER, blue stones, e.g. amethyst, turquoise, sapphire, jasper, blue diamond.
>
> With VENUS, green stones, e.g., the emerald and some kinds of sapphires.
>
> With SATURN, black stones, e.g., jet, onyx, obsidian, diamond, and black coral.[18]

This is not the only tradition that associates gemstone crystals with certain planets.

In the Old Testament, there is a very tight association of specific tribes of Israel, the twelve sons of Jacob, not only with certain gemstones, but as there are twelve such sons or

---

[18] Sir E.A. Wallis-Budge, *Amulets and Superstitions: The Original Texts with Translations and Descriptions of a Long Series of Egyptian, Sumerian, Assyruan, Hebrew, Christian, Gnostic and Muslin Amulets and Talismans and Magical Figures, with Chapters on the Evil Eye, The Origin of the Amulet, the Pentagon, the Swastika, the Cross (Pagan and Chrstian), the Properties of Stone, Rings, Divination, Numbers, the Kabbalah, Ancient Astrology etc.* (Oxford: Oxford University Press, 1930 Kessinger Publishing Reprint. ISBN 0-7661-5789-X), p. 423, cited in my *The Cosmic War: Interplanetary Warfare, Modern Physics, and Ancient Texts* (Kempton, Illinois: Adventures Unlimited Press, 2007, ISBN 978-1-931882-75-0), p. 244.

tribes, with the twelve houses of the Zodiac. As we shall discover in a moment, there is also a very suggestive association of these gemstones with the guardian angels of certain tribes and nations, and with one in particular.

There are three passages in the book of Genesis which detail the order of birth of Jacob's sons, who will become the fathers—and names—of the twelve tribes of Israel:

1) *in Genesis 29:31-35* Jacob's wife Leah bears *Reuben, Simeon, Levi*, and *Judah;*
2) *in Genesis 30:6-22* Jacob's wife's Rachel's maid, Billah, bears *Dan,* and *Naphthali*, while Leah's maid Zilpah bears *Gad*, and *Asher* while Leah herself bears *Issachar, Zebulon,* a daughter, Dinah, and finally *Joseph;* and finally,
3) *in Genesis 35:18* Rachel bears *Benjamin.*[19]

In Exodus 28:15-21, these twelve sons or tribes are in turn each represented by one of the gemstones on the Hebrew high priest's breastplate, or *ephod*:

> And thou shalt make the breastplate of judgment with cunning work; after the work of the ephod thou shalt make it; of gold, of blue, and of purple, and of scarlet, and of fine twined linen, shalt thou make it. Foursquare it shall be being double; a span shall be the length thereof, and a span shall be the breadth thereof. And thou shalt set in it settings of stones, even four rows or stones: the first row shall be a sardius, a topaz, and a carbuncle; this shall be the first row. And the second row shall be an emerald, a sapphire, and a diamond. And the third row a ligue, an agate, and an amethyst. And the fourth row shall be a beryl, and an onyx, and a jasper; they shall be set in gold in their inclosings.

[19] All references to and citations of the Bible are from the Authorized King James version.

> And the stones shall be with the names of the children of Israel, twelve, according to their names, like the engravings of a signet; every one with his name shall they be according to the twelve tribes.

The phrase "according to their names, like the engravings of a signet" is a strong clue that the breastplate of judgment had to do with governance, for a signet ring is a symbol of a governing authority often engraved with the personal arms or seal of that person or his office. In the western church, for example, clergy, and particularly bishops or other members of the hierarchy, wear rings as part of their vestiture of office, and these are often either of a precious stone or amethyst or sapphire, or engraved with a seal for use on wax sealing important documents.

Thus we have the following association of tribes and gemstones

Reuben *Carnelian*	Simeon *Topaz*	Levi *Emerald*
Judah *Green Feldspar*	Dan *Sapphire*	Naphthali *Diamond*
Gad *Zircon*	Asher *Agate*	Issachar *Amethyst*
Zebulon *Beryl*	Joseph *Onyx*	Benjamin *Jasper*

The stones of the Hebrew High Priest's Ephod,
Or Breastplate of Judgment

Given the association of crystals with plasmas, and the thesis of Robert Temple that plasmas in turn represent a kind of bodiless inorganic intelligent life form, then this table also perhaps represents a continuation of the tradition mentioned by St. John of Damascus that various nations and regions of the planet have their own kind of "guardians" or angelic overseers who are represented by the crystals that "transduce" or "invoke" them.

But what of the Damascene's statement that the governing angelic power of this planet, planet Earth, was the leader of the fallen angelic host? Is there anything indicating this?

Indeed there is, and the parallel with the Hebrew high priest's "breastplate of judgment" is there for all to see in the description of Lucifer's crown given in the book of Ezekiel. Here the passage in question begins with a reference to the King of Tyre, but quickly passes to a passage about the governance of the globe, which most biblical scholars agree is a passage about Lucifer:

> Son of man, take up a lamentation upon the king of Tyrus, and say unto him, Thus saith the Lord GOD; Thou sealest up the sum, full of wisdom, and perfect in beauty. Thou hast been in Eden the garden of God; every precious stone was thy covering, sardius, topaz, and the diamond, the beryl, the onyx, and the jasper, the sapphire, the emerald, and the carbuncle, and gold: the workmanship of thy tabrets and of thy pipes was prepared in thee in the day that thou was created. Thou are the anointed cherub that covereth; and I have set thee so thou wast upon the holy mountain of God; thou hast walked up and down in the midst of the stones of fire. Thou wast perfect in thy ways from the day that thou wast created, till iniquity was found in thee. By the multitude of thy merchandise they have filled the midst of thee with violence, and thou hast sinned: therefore I will cast thee as profane out of the mountain of God: and I will destroy thee, O covering cherub, from the midst of the stones of fire. Thine heart was lifted up because of thy beauty, thou hast corrupted thy wisdom by reason of thy brightness: I will cast thee to the ground, I will lay thee before kings, that they may behold thee. Thou hast defiled thy sanctuaries by the multitude of thine iniquities, by the

> iniquity of thy traffic; therefore will I bring forth a fire from the midst of thee, it shall devour thee, and I will bring thee to ashes upon the earth in the sight of all them that behold thee. All they that know thee among the people shall be astonished at thee: thou shalt be a terror, and never shalt thou be any more.[20]

Notice how closely this passage parallels that of the *Ludlul Bel Nimeqi*, with the association of a demon and a mountain, and, in this particular case, the fact that the demon walks "up and down in the midst of the stones of fire," which, if the formula *ekur=mountain=mountain house=planet* holds true, would be yet another possible oblique reference to the Grand Gallery of the Great Pyramid, and the crystalline resonators which I have hypothesized might once have lined the chamber, and which Sitchin himself viewed as the rainbow of crystals in that part of the structure. To put as sharp a point as possible on it, certain passages both of Mesopotamian and of biblical texts seem to point to the association of demons with pyramids and to crystals, an association that begins to make sense if the plasma life hypothesis is true. Indeed, the passage from Ezekiel might even be referring *directly* to that hypothesis with its reference to pipes and tabrets, a reference

---

[20] Ezekiel 28:12-19. For two typical early Christian commentaries on this passage attributing the focus, not to the King of Tyre, but to Lucifer, see Origen, *De Principiis*, trans. and ed. Rev. Frederick Crombie, D.D., *Ante-Nicene Fathers,* Alexander Roberts, D.D., James Donaldson, LL.D., A; Cleveland Coxe, D.D. *Vol. 4: Tertullian (IV), Minucius Felix, Commodian, Origen* (Peabody, Massachusetts: Hendrickson Publishers, Inc. 2004, ISBN 1-56563-086-6), p. 258; and Tertullian, *Against Marcion*, X, trans. Peter Holmes, *Ante-Nicene Fathers,* Alexander Roberts, D.D., James Donaldson, LL.D., A; Cleveland Coxe, D.D. *Vol.3: Tertullian, Parts I,II, & III* ((Peabody, Massachusetts: Hendrickson Publishers, Inc. 2004, ISBN 1-56563-085-8), p. 306.

typical of musical instruments, also typical to organisms, for tabrets are just an old word for "membrane," and we have already seen that plasmas have their own peculiar types of pipes and tabrets with their filaments and double layers, layers which, as we have also seen, are acoustic membranes and oscillators.

Note that two of these stones—diamond and onyx—could be considered "white" and "black," that is, as reflecting or absorbing all other frequencies, while the rest of the stones cover the range from high frequency (sapphires and blue) to lower frequencies (emeralds and green, carbuncles and red, topaz and yellow, and so on). This would suggest a kind of governance or power over and in all frequencies, a symbolism appropriate for the governing "plasma guardian" of an entire planet and its inhabitants.

There is more, however, for if one examines the stones of this "cherub that covereth," they turn out to be none other than *the majority of stones on the high priest's breastplate of judgment*: sardius, topaz, diamond, sapphire, emerald, and carbuncle: the "cherub that covereth" is missing the stones of the third row of the high priest's *ephod* or breastplate of judgement, the stones belonging to Gad, Asher, and Issachar, which is to say, the zircon, agate, and amethyst:

Rueben *Carnelian*	Simeon *Topaz*	Levi *Emerald*
Judah *Green Feldspar*	Dan *Sapphire*	Naphthali *Diamond*
Zebulon *Beryl*	Joseph *Onyx*	Benjamin *Jasper*

The stones of Lucifer's Ephod,
Which is missing the third row from the High Priest's ephod

Gad *Zircon*	Asher *Agate*	Issachar *Amethyst*

The Missing Third Row of the High Priest's ephod which is not found in Lucifer's Ephod

In the 49th chapter of Genesis, Jacob calls all of his sons together to give prophecies over each of them. Those concerning Gad, Asher, and Issachar have long been the source of commentary from Christian commentators, with respect to the missing stones of Lucifer's ephod:

> Issachar is a strong ass couching down between two burdens: and he saw that rest was good, and the land that it was pleasant; and bowed his shoulder to bear, and became a servant unto tribute…
>
> …Gad, a troop shall overcome him, but he shall overcome at the last.
>
> Out of Asher his bread shall be fat, and he shall yield royal dainties.[21]

The "burden of Issachar" which he bowed to bear has been understood by Christian commentators to refer to Christ and the burden of the Cross, Gad's troop the Roman soldier-executioners, and the "royal dainties" of Asher as Christ himself. By omitting these stones from Lucifer's ephod, the symbolism becomes clear: Lucifer will never have a royal heir, will never carry anyone's burden, and will never overcome anything but is overcome.

Or to put a much finer point on it once again, Lucifer's governance is fatally flawed since it is entirely narcissistic and for his own benefit.

---

[21] Genesis 49: 14-15, 19-20.

Thus, the association of plasmas and crystals that we surveyed in the previous chapter combines with the lore of angels from the Old Testament and the Damascene to produce an interesting series of broader implications and rationalizations. The "transmutative aether" of the ancient cosmic war, or of the 19th century physicists' *aether lumeniferous*, becomes the "super-fine" matter of a plasma capable of shapeshifting, and of penetrating other matter.[22] Crystals themselves, since they grow in a particular geometry of space-time and gravitational and electromagnetic forces have lattice structures reflective of, and resonant to, that geometry. They thus constitute not only *resonators* of that geometry, but if there were an adequately developed science of the historiography of crystal lattices, they would then also constitute *biographies* and hence *invokers or transducers* of those plasmas; small wonder, then, that the "Tablets of Destinies" may not only have been crystals, but were only activated biometrically, by being in close proximity to, or in the actual physical possession of, the "gods" who wielded them.[23] Once again, the hypothesis of intelligent plasma life is both highly suggestive, and highly unifying across a set of otherwise disjointed and separate elements.

c. Edgar Cayce's "Terrible Mighty Crystal"

There is yet another association of crystals with the power of a Very High Civilization in the mists of pre-history. In Edgar Cayce's "reading" on Atlantis, we learn of the

---

[22] See my *The Cosmic War*, pp. 250-254. If the plasma intelligent life hypothesis be true, then this ability of plasmas to penetrate other matter may also constitute a physical basis for the phenomenon of demonic possession.

[23] See my *The Cosmic War*, pp. 254, 269-270.

possibility of a "terrible mighty crystal"[24] that was the source of Atlantean power, a crystal that, moreover, had to be "prepared" in Cayce's words, that is to say, synthesized or grown or "prepared" in some other way. The "preparation of this stone," he notes, "was solely in the hands of the initiates at the time; and the entity was among those who directed the influences of the radiation which arose, in the form of rays that were invisible to the eye by acted upon the stones themselves as set in the motivating forces..."[25] While Cayce's readings are always somewhat opaque to any conventional interpretation, and while the term "entity" which so often occurs in his readings is one of those terms whose meaning seems to vary depending on the context of (or person requesting!) the reading, in this instance it minimally indicates that some "entity" was actually directing the radiations from the stones, which presumably included the "terrible mighty crystal." That "entity" could be the individual requesting the reading, or another kind of "entity" altogether, perhaps even Sitchin's "demon in the ekur."

The most profoundly disturbing thing in this series of readings, however, is the following suggestive passage, and note how the editor—Hugh Lynn Cayce—introduces it in the 1968 book which we have been referencing:

> The next paragraph sounds like a description of a magnetic bottle for containing hot plasma or a giant laser.
>
> "As for a description of the manner of construction of the stone: we find it was a large cylindrical glass (as would be termed today); *cut with facets in such manner that the capstone on top of it made for centralizing the power or force that concentrated between the end of the cylinder and*

---

[24] Edgar Evans Cayce, *Edgar Cayce on Atlantis* (New York: Haethorne Books, Inc., 1968, no ISBN), p. 87.

[25] Ibid., p. 89.

> *the capstone itself.* As indicated, *the records as to ways of constructing same are in three places in the earth, as it stands today: in the sunken portion of Atlantis, or Poseidia,* where a portion of the temples may yet be discovered under the slime of ages of sea water—*near what is known as Bimini, off the coast of Florida. And (secondly) in the temple records that were in Egypt, where the entity acted later in cooperation with others towards preserving the records that came from the land where these had been kept. Also (thirdly) the records that were carried to what is now Yucatan, in America, where these stones (which they know so little about) are now—during the last few months—being uncovered."*
>
> I interpret this last paragraph to mean that some part of a building or temple in Yucatan had an emblem, drawing, or carving of one of these crystals (or firestones) on it. Probably, in 1933, an archeological expedition was engaged in transporting portions of the temple or building stones to the U.S. Possibly, even now, the carving or drawing is reposing unrecognized in the basement of some museum.[26]

Possibly Cayce was referring to the discoveries associated with the crystal skulls which were taking place at more or less the approximate time referred to in the reading, and in the case of the Mitchell-Hedges skull, which were found in the Yucatan region. What *is* highly suggestive are the clear connections of this "terrible mighty crystal" to Egypt, and according to the editor, the suggestive resemblance of this crystal both to plasma and the optical cavity of a laser.

[26] Edgar Evans Cayce, *Edgar Cayce on Atlantis*, pp. 90-91, emphasis added.

D. Extension, Entanglement, and Retrocausation: A Reconsideration of the "Grandfather Paradox"

Thus far we have been primarily concerned with aspects of the intelligent plasma life hypothesis having to do with extension in space, though in advancing the hypothesis that the lattice structure of crystals is a response to their growth under certain geometric configurations of physical forces we have also implied the notion of extension in time, we now turn more explicitly to that concept in order to unfold a series of implications that seem to emerge from a consideration of the extension of plasmas over vast stretches of time. Let us begin by assuming that the massive plasma structure called the Sloan Great Wall, the plasma structure that is 1.37 *billion light years* long, is also an intelligent living plasma. How is such a structure even held together? Such questions have led many scientists to postulate that life itself *depends* upon the quantum phenomena of non-locality, entanglement, and "tunneling" and that the whole notion of individual consciousness itself is "non-local."

Once such vast extent both in space and in time to a life-form is granted, tremendous age and antiquity is not far behind, and with the notion of crystals and entanglement comes the implication that such plasmas might be special kinds of time crystals, able to influence events not only in distant space, but distant futures, or pasts. Here again, author and researcher Robert Temple has put forward a multitude of speculative hypotheses that are worth some consideration, this time not in regard to plasmas as intelligent life, but with respect to the Chinese system of divination called the *I Ching* its implication that *events* also have a discrete *structure*.[27]

[27] Robert Temple, *Netherworld: Discovering the Oracle of the Dead and Ancient Techniques of Foretelling the Future* (London: Century, 1988, ISBN 0-7126-8404-2), pp. 334-335. It is worth

This structure in turn itself is crystal-like and plasma-like in structure, with discrete pathways (filaments) and regions (cells, nodes,):

> What I propose is that events which are in the process of changing drastically, of coming to fruition—of giving birth, as it were—manifest similar connecting links with 'event-cells' far distant as well as near, and that some geometrical or structural 'crystallizations' occur when this happens. Such forces may possibly affect material objects within the 'event-fields' in which they are operating, leading to cracking or other phenomena of that kind. And I believe we cannot rule out that 'event-fields' may influence physical processes or material objects such as the sorting of yarrow stalks or the cracking of bones and shells by heat. In other words, there may well be a thoroughly respectable and scientific basis for the occasional or even frequent accuracy of traditional Chinese divinatory techniques.[28]

Temple even goes so far as to suggest that events have their own topology, and calls synchronicities such as divination a "higher order event," i.e., an event whose *pattern and lattice-work of pathways and nodes* resembles *other* events. Event pathways thus resemble those patterns that topologists and other mathematicians call "tessellations," they are *arrays* and *sets* of information.[29]

---

noting that on p. 360 of that work, Temple reproduces a diagram of the double membrane of a living biological cell and noting its similarity to double layers in plasmas. He had to wait about 3 more decades before the physics of plasmas advanced sufficiently enough to bear the weight of forming the intelligent plasma life hypothesis.

[28] Robert Temple, *Netherworld*, p. 363

[29] Ibid., pp. 370, 390, 399.

Viewing events as *sets of information, each element of which is derived by multiple complex pathways* goes a long way to explaining why retrocausation is not only possible, but how the "grandfather paradox" might be avoided. We all know what the "grandfather paradox" is; it is a kind of *Oedipus* complex involving time travel: suppose we travel back in time, meet our own grandfather (paternal or maternal is never specified) and, not recognizing him, we cause his death before he, in turn, can sire our mother or father, and they, in turn, us. What happens then? One school of thought says that because the paradox itself is the result, that time travel is impossible, and hence the paradox cannot arise in the first place. Another school holds that time travel is possible, but that in causing the death of one's own grandfather, one also erases oneself, and a whole new timeline of events emerges, without you *or* your grandfather (and presumably one of your parents).

In other words, the timeline, and *each event in it*, is viewed in a linear fashion, with each event being a mere node or point, thusly:

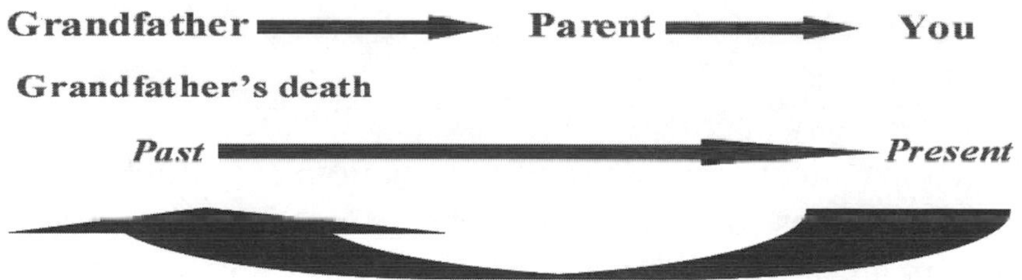

Viewed as components in *events*, both your parents, grandparents, and you, are the results of very limited biological and genetic pathways.

But let us now consider a problem—not so much for the grandfather paradox—*but for the linear (and incidentally, very materialistic) thinking that produced it*: twins, and doppelgängers. In the case of identical twins, we're familiar with how 'entangled" such persons can be, and yet at the same time, how very different their persons can often be. Similarly, we're familiar with the phenomenon of the doppelgänger, an individual with no immediate biological or genetic relationship to another individual, and yet who looks and oftentimes behaves so similarly that mistakes are often made between them, with the mistake oftentimes being the assumption that the individual and his or her doppelgänger are siblings. Now plug these phenomena into *events*, and what results is something intriguing: any event involving a certain person can have an "event harmonic" where that certain person, as an element in the set comprising that event, is replaced by another person that is a doppelgänger (or harmonic!) of that person. The resulting event is *nearly the same*, and more importantly, the paradox grows *fainter* the *further back* one goes. Suppose you travel back and somehow cause the death, not of your grandfather, but of a great-great-great-grandfather. The pathways in time from then to *you* might not be exactly the same, but *you* (or a close "harmonic" thereof!) may still arise.

We may perhaps put this in the form of a more "mathematical" analogy and speculation: the closer in order of derivatives (or in time) two events are, the more *difficult* it is for the lower order derivative to retrocausively influence the higher, and the farther apart or more distant in order of derivatives (or time) two events are, the easier it is for the lower to retrocausively influence the higher. The closer in order of derivatives the two are, the more probable is the occurrence of a paradox.[30]

E. Some Concluding Caveats

We have not, of course, *proven* that plasmas are alive and intelligent. We have merely shown that the idea of a "very fine matter" that might be an inorganic and intelligent life form is not all that new, and that *when* one assumes it, many disparate and seemingly unconnected areas and problems are suddenly resolved and connected in a very deep way. With respect to the idea of ancient wars of the gods and men, or of the Great Pyramid Weapon Hypothesis, the wars are no longer metaphors for plasma discharges and an "electric universe" model, but the latter—the discharges and the model—are merely signs that real persons, real intelligences with all the vast power of the gods that ancient myths attribute to them, are *real* and fought *real* wars of truly *cosmic* extent. Neither the powers, nor the gods, are metaphorical. They are very, very *real*, and very, *very* dangerous.

It's small wonder, therefore, that "foo fighters" and "ball lightning" and "balls of fire" started showing up in mass numbers near the end of World War Two—or more recently when tethers on space shuttles broke after an electrical surge, and little balls in their hundreds and thousands showed up on camera to seemingly "inspect" what had happened after an absence of some millennia, when mankind, in the form of the

---

[30] Another speculative implication that arises from these hypotheses is germane to the plasma life hypothesis, and this must be thought about long and hard: these two "laws" are also another way of saying that if plasmas are alive and intelligent, then they are more likely to be of great antiquity than not.

Nazis, the Americans, and the Imperial Japanese were on the cusp of, and eventually intruded into, that plasma realm, when they detonated their own artificial plasma-creators… the atom bomb….[31]

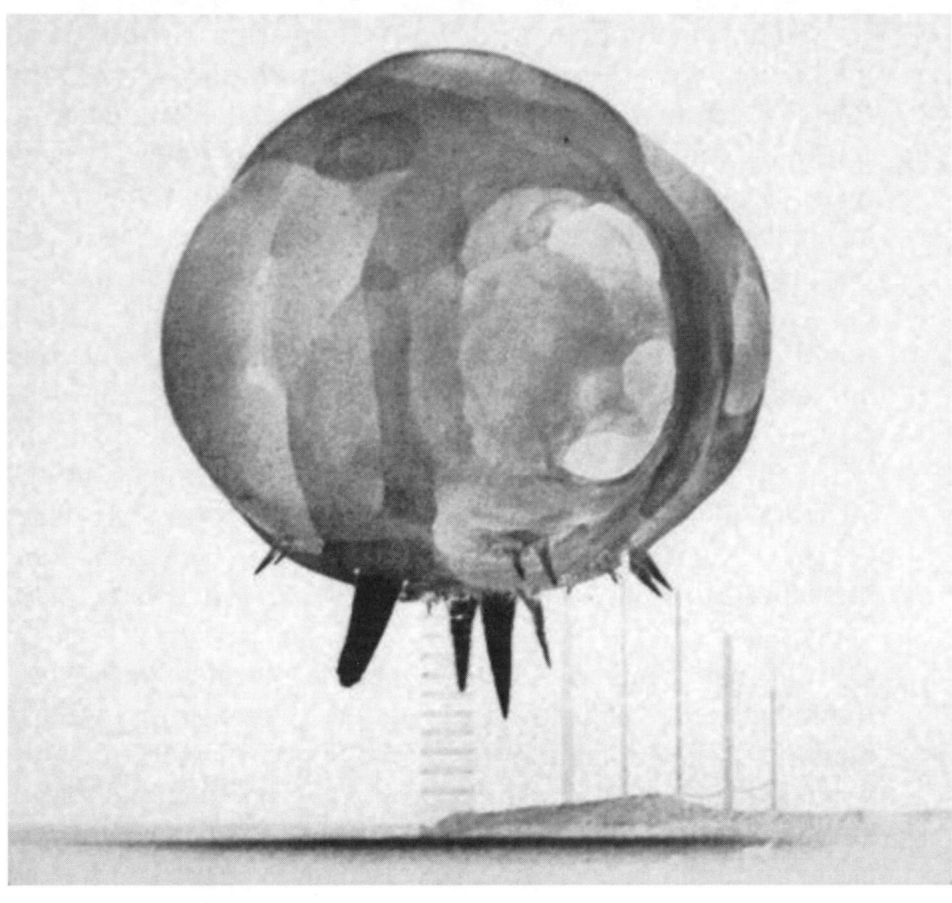

[31] And yes, you read that correctly: the Nazis and the imperial Japanese both also likely detonated their own A-bombs shortly before the end of World War Two. See my *Reich of the Black Sun* for that story. From *The Giza Death Star*, to the Reich, to the *Demon in the Ekur*, it's all related, folks…

BIBLIOGRAPHY

No author. "Ekur." *Wikipedia.*

Alfvén, Hannes. *Cosmic Plasma*, Astrophysics and Space Science Library, Volume 82. Dordrecht, Holland. D. Reidel Publishing Company. 1981. 978-94-009-8376-2.

Alfvén, Hannes. *Cosmical Electrodynamics*. Oxford. 1950. ISBN 978-1541348400 (Reprint).

Cade, C. Maxwell, and Davis, Delphine. *The Taming of the Thunderbolts: The Science and Superstition of Ball Lightning*. London. Abelard-Schuman. 1969. (Obsolete Standard Book Number 200-71531-3.)

Cayce, Edgar Evans. *Edgar Cayce on Atlantis*. New York. Hawthorn Books, Inc. (W.Clement Stone, Publisher). 1968. No ISBN.

Chopra, Deepak, and Kafatos, Menas C., Eds. *Quantum Physics, Retrocausation, PreCognition, Entanglement, Consciousness, Mental Time Travel.* Cambridge, Massachusetts. Cosmology Science Publishers. 2015. ISBN 978-1-938-024-48-1.

Dionysius the Areopagite. *Pseudo-Dionysius: The Complete Works: Classics of Western Spirituality*. Trans. Colm Luibheid. New York. Paulist Press. 1987. ISBN 0-8091-2838-1.

Farrell, Joseph P. *The Cosmic War: Interplanetary Warfare, Modern Physics and Ancient Text: A Study in Non-Catastrophist Interpretations of Ancient Legends*. Kempton, Illinois. Adventures Unlimited Press. 2007. ISBN 978-1-931-882-75-0.

Farrell, Joseph P. *Covert Wars and Breakaway Civilizations: The Secret Space Program, Celestial Psyops, and Hidden*

Conflicts. Kempton, Illinois. Adventures Unlimited Press. 2012. ISBN 978-1-935487-83-8.

Farrell, Joseph P. *The Giza Death Star Deployed.* Corviss Reprint, 2022.www.Lulu.com.

Farrell, Joseph P. *The Giza Death Star Destroyed.* Corviss Reprint, 2022. www.Lulu.com

Farrell, Joseph P. *The Giza Death Star Revisited: An Updated Revision of the Weapon Hypothesis of the Great Pyramid.* Kempton, Illinois. Adventures Unlimited Press. 2023. ISBN 978-1-948803-57-1.

Farrell, Joseph P. *The Giza Death Star.* Corviss Press Reprint, 2022. www.Lulu.com.

Farrell, Joseph P., with DeHart, Scott D. *The Grid of the Gods: The Aftermath of the Cosmic War and the Physics of the Pyramid Peoples*. Kempton, Illinois. Adventures Unlimited Press. 2011. ISBN 978-1-935487-39-5.

Fernandez, Elizabeth. "Brain Experiment Suggests that Consciousness relies on Quantum Entanglement." Bigthink.com/hard-science/brain-consciousness-quantum-entanglement/

Foster, Benjamin R., trans. and ed. *Before the Muses: An Anthology of Akkadian Literature*. Bethesda, Maryland. CDL Press. 2005. ISBN 978-1-883053-76-5.

Gober, Mark. *An End to Upside Down Thinking: Dispelling the Myths that the Brain Produces Consciousness, and the Implications for Everyday Life.* Cardiff-by-the-Sea, California. 2018. ISBN 978-1-947637-85-6.

Greene, Tristan. "Scientists think Quantum Tunneling in Space led to Life on Earth." March 7, 2022. thenextweb.com/news/scientists-thin-quantum-tunneling-in-space-lef-life-on-earth

Hall, Manley P. *The Secret Teachings of All Ages: Masonic, Hermetic, Qabbalistic & Rosicrucian Symbolical Philosophy, Being an Interpretation of the Secret*

Teachings Concealed within the Rituals, Allegories and Mysteries of all Ages. Los Angeles, California. The Philosophical Research Society, Inc., Diamond Jubilee Edition Reduced Facsimile. 1988. ISBN 978-0-89314-548-4.

Hamer, Ashl;ey. "Entangled Quantum Particles can 'Communicate' through Time." www. discovery. Com / science/Entangled-Quantum-Particles-Communicate

Lenzi, Alan. "Translation of *Ludlul Bel Nemeqi.*" scholarlycommons.pacific.edu/cgi/viewcontent/cgi?article =1189&context=cop-facbooks.

Levi-Civitta, Tullio. "On the Analytic Expression that must be given to the Gravitational Tensor in Einstein's Theory." arXiv:physics/9906004v1 [physics.hist-ph) 2 June 1999.

Lovejoy, Arthur O. *The Great Chain of Being*. Cembridge, Massachusetts. Harvard University Press. 1964. ISBN 0-674-36153-9.

MacIsaac, Tara. "A New Theory of Consciousness: The Mind Exists as a Field Connected to the Brain." www.scienceandnonduality.com/article/a-new-theory-of-consciouness-the-mind-exists-as-a-field-connected-to-the-brain

Mann, Adam. "Is the Sun a Node in a Gigantic Alien Space Internet? Scientists scanned the Skies to Check." www.livescience.com/sun-alien-gravitational-wave-network.

Moskowitz, Clara. "Weird! Quantum Entanglement Can Reach into the Past." www.livescience.com/19975-spooky-quantum-entanglement.html

Peat, F. David. *Infinite Potential: The Life and Times of David Bohm.* Perseus/Basic Books. 1997. ISBN 978-0201328202.

Peratt, Anthony L. *Physics of the Plasma Universe, Second Edition.* New York. Springer Verlag. 2015. ISBN 978-1-4939-3694-6.

Piazzi-Smyth, Charles, F.R.E.S., F.R.A.S. *The Great Pyramid: Its Secrets and Mysteries Revealed.* New York. Bell Publishing. No Date. Reprint of the 1880 edition *Our Inheritance in the Great Pyramid.* ISBN 0-517-26403-X.

Pochan, André. L'Énigme de las Grande Pyramide. Paris: Editions Robert Laffont, 6 place Saint-Sulpice, Paris-6a. 1971. No ISBN.

Pylkkänen, Paavo. *Mind, Matter, and the Implicate Order.* Berlin. Springer Verlag. 2007. ISBN 3-540-23891-3.

Silverman, Jacob. "Are we looking for aliens n the wrong places?" science.howstuffowkrs.com/weird-life.htm.

Sitchin, Zecharia. *The Wars of Gods and Men.* Book Three of *The Earth Chronicles*. Santa Fe. Bear and Company Publishing. 1985. 978-093968090-4.

St. John of Damascus, *On the Orthodox Faith (De Fide Orthodoxa*), trans. from the Greek and ed., Rev. S.D.F. Salmond, D.D., F.E.I.S., *Nicene and Post-Nicene Fathers,* Vol. IX, *Hilary of Poitiers, John of Damascus.* Grand Rapids, Michigan: Wm. B. Eerdmans Publishing Company. 1997.

Temple, Robert. *A New Science of Heaven: How the Science of Plasma Changes our Understanding of Physical and Spiritual Reality*. Falkirk, Stirlingshire. Coronet. 2021. ISBN 978-1-473-62374-3.

Temple, Robert. *Netherworld: Discovering the Oracle of the Dead and Ancient Techniques of Foretelling the Future*. Chatham, Kent. Random House, U.K./ Century. 2002. ISBN 978-0-7126-8404-2.

Tsytovich, V.N., Morfill, G.E., Fortov, V.E., Gusein-Zade, N.G., Klumov, B.A., Vladimirov, S.V. "From Plasma Crystals and Helical Structures towards Inorganic Living Matter." *New Journal of Physics,* 9, 2007, 263,

Get these fascinating books from your nearest bookstore or directly from: Adventures Unlimited Press

www.adventuresunlimitedpress.com

COVERT WARS AND BREAKAWAY CIVILIZATIONS
By Joseph P. Farrell

Farrell delves into the creation of breakaway civilizations by the Nazis in South America and other parts of the world. He discusses the advanced technology that they took with them at the end of the war and the psychological war that they waged for decades on America and NATO. He investigates the secret space programs currently sponsored by the breakaway civilizations and the current militaries in control of planet Earth. Plenty of astounding accounts, documents and speculation on the incredible alternative history of hidden conflicts and secret space programs that began when World War II officially "ended."

292 Pages. 6x9 Paperback. Illustrated. $19.95. Code: BCCW

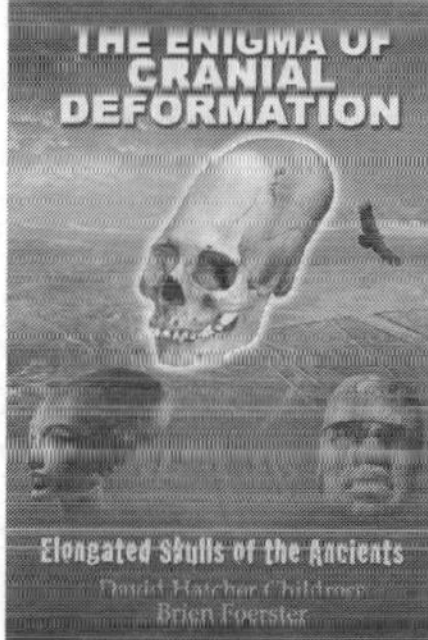

THE ENIGMA OF CRANIAL DEFORMATION
Elongated Skulls of the Ancients
By David Hatcher Childress and Brien Foerster

In a book filled with over a hundred astonishing photos and a color photo section, Childress and Foerster take us to Peru, Bolivia, Egypt, Malta, China, Mexico and other places in search of strange elongated skulls and other cranial deformation. The puzzle of why diverse ancient people—even on remote Pacific Islands—would use head-binding to create elongated heads is mystifying. Where did they even get this idea? Did some people naturally look this way—with long narrow heads? Were they some alien race? Were they an elite race that roamed the entire planet? Why do anthropologists rarely talk about cranial deformation and know so little about it? Color Section.

250 Pages. 6x9 Paperback. Illustrated. $19.95. Code: ECD

THE GIZA DEATH STAR REVISITED
An Updated Revision of the Weapon Hypothesis of the Great Pyramid
By Joseph P. Farrell

A summary, revision, and update of his original *Giza Death Star* trilogy in this one-volume compendium of the argument, the physics, and the all-important ancient texts, from the Edfu Temple texts to the Lugal-e and the Enuma Elish that he believes may have made the Great Pyramid a tremendously powerful weapon of mass destruction. Those texts, Farrell argues, provide the clues to the powerful physics of longitudinal waves in the medium that only began to be unlocked centuries later by Sir Isaac Newton and his well-known studies of the Great Pyramid, and even later by Nikola Tesla's "electro-acoustic" experiments. Chapters and sections include: A Remarkable, and Remarkably Strange, Structure; The Hypothesized Functions of the Great Pyramid's Topological-Analogical Code of Ancient Texts; Greaves, Gravity, and Newton; Meta-Materials, Crystals, and Torsion; The Top Secret Cold War Soviet Pyramid Research, and much, much more!

360 Pages. 6x9 Paperback. Illustrated.. $19.95. Code: GDSR

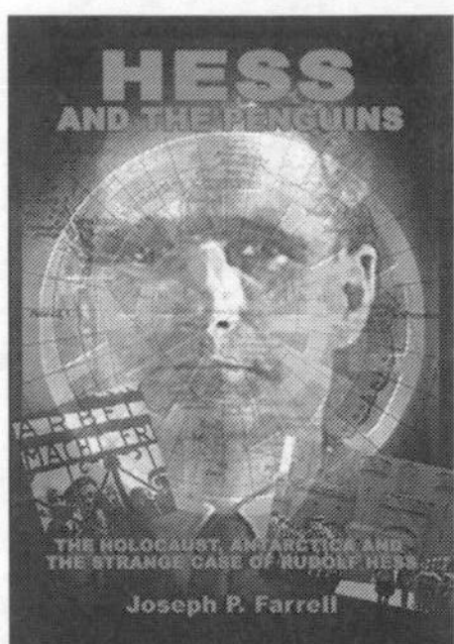

HESS AND THE PENGUINS

The Holocaust, Antarctica and the Strange Case of Rudolf Hess

By Joseph P. Farrell

Farrell looks at Hess' mission to make peace with Britain and get rid of Hitler—even a plot to fly Hitler to Britain for capture! How much did Göring and Hitler know of Rudolf Hess' subversive plot, and what happened to Hess? Why was a doppleganger put in Spandau Prison and then "suicided"? Did the British use an early form of mind control on Hess' double? John Foster Dulles of the OSS and CIA suspected as much. Farrell also uncovers the strange death of Admiral Richard Byrd's son in 1988, about the same time of the death of Hess.

288 Pages. 6x9 Paperback. Illustrated. $19.95. Code: HAPG

HIDDEN FINANCE, ROGUE NETWORKS & SECRET SORCERY

The Fascist International, 9/11, & Penetrated Operations

By Joseph P. Farrell

Farrell investigates the theory that there were not *two* levels to the 9/11 event, but *three*. He says that the twin towers were downed by the force of an exotic energy weapon, one similar to the Tesla energy weapon suggested by Dr. Judy Wood, and ties together the tangled web of missing money, secret technology and involvement of portions of the Saudi royal family. Farrell unravels the many layers behind the 9-11 attack, layers that include the Deutschebank, the Bush family, the German industrialist Carl Duisberg, Saudi Arabian princes and the energy weapons developed by Tesla before WWII.

296 Pages. 6x9 Paperback. Illustrated. $19.95. Code: HFRN

THRICE GREAT HERMETICA & THE JANUS AGE

By Joseph P. Farrell

What do the Fourth Crusade, the exploration of the New World, secret excavations of the Holy Land, and the pontificate of Innocent the Third all have in common? Answer: Venice and the Templars. What do they have in common with Jesus, Gottfried Leibniz, Sir Isaac Newton, Rene Descartes, and the Earl of Oxford? Answer: Egypt and a body of doctrine known as Hermeticism. The hidden role of Venice and Hermeticism reached far and wide, into the plays of Shakespeare (a.k.a. Edward DeVere, Earl of Oxford), into the quest of the three great mathematicians of the Early Enlightenment for a lost form of analysis, and back into the end of the classical era, to little known Egyptian influences at work during the time of Jesus.

354 Pages. 6x9 Paperback. Illustrated. $19.95. Code: TGHJ

REICH OF THE BLACK SUN

Nazi Secret Weapons & the Cold War Allied Legend

by Joseph P. Farrell

Why were the Allies worried about an atom bomb attack by the Germans in 1944? Why did the Soviets threaten to use poison gas against the Germans? Why did Hitler in 1945 insist that holding Prague could win the war for the Third Reich? Why did US General George Patton's Third Army race for the Skoda works at Pilsen in Czechoslovakia instead of Berlin? Why did the US Army not test the uranium atom bomb it dropped on Hiroshima? Why did the Luftwaffe fly a non-stop round trip mission to within twenty miles of New York City in 1944? Farrel takes the reader on a scientific-historical journey in order to answer these questions. Arguing that Nazi Germany won the race for the atom bomb in late 1944,

352 PAGES. 6x9 PAPERBACK. ILLUSTRATED. $16.95. CODE: ROBS

THE COSMIC WAR
Interplanetary Warfare, Modern Physics, and Ancient Texts
By Joseph P. Farrell

There is ample evidence across our solar system of catastrophic events. The asteroid belt may be the remains of an exploded planet! The known planets are scarred from incredible impacts, and teeter in their orbits due to causes heretofore inadequately explained. Included: The history of the Exploded Planet hypothesis, and what mechanism can actually explode a planet. The role of plasma cosmology, plasma physics and scalar physics. The ancient texts telling of such destructions: from Sumeria (Tiamat's destruction by Marduk), Egypt (Edfu and the Mars connections), Greece (Saturn's role in the War of the Titans) and the ancient Americas.

436 Pages. 6x9 Paperback. Illustrated.. $18.95. Code: COSW

THE GRID OF THE GODS
The Aftermath of the Cosmic War & the Physics of the Pyramid Peoples
By Joseph P. Farrell with Scott D. de Hart

Farrell looks at Ashlars and Engineering; Anomalies at the Temples of Angkor; The Ancient Prime Meridian: Giza; Transmitters, Nazis and Geomancy; the Lithium-7 Mystery; Nazi Transmitters and the Earth Grid; The Master Plan of a Hidden Elite; Moving and Immoveable Stones; Uncountable Stones and Stones of the Giants and Gods; The Grid and the Ancient Elite; Finding the Center of the Land; The Ancient Catastrophe, the Very High Civilization, and the Post-Catastrophe Elite; Tiahuanaco and the Puma Punkhu Paradox: Ancient Machining; The Black Brotherhood and Blood Sacrifices; The Gears of Giza: the Center of the Machine; tons more.

436 Pages. 6x9 Paperback. Illustrated. $19.95. Code: GOG

THE SS BROTHERHOOD OF THE BELL
The Nazis' Incredible Secret Technology
by Joseph P. Farrell

In 1945, a mysterious Nazi secret weapons project code-named "The Bell" left its underground bunker in lower Silesia, along with all its project documentation, and a four-star SS general named Hans Kammler. Taken aboard a massive six engine Junkers 390 ultra-long range aircraft, "The Bell," Kammler, and all project records disappeared completely, along with the gigantic aircraft. It is thought to have flown to America or Argentina. What was "The Bell"? What new physics might the Nazis have discovered with it? How far did the Nazis go after the war to protect the advanced energy technology that it represented?

456 pages. 6x9 Paperback. Illustrated. $16.95. Code: SSBB

THE THIRD WAY
The Nazi International, European Union, & Corporate Fascism
By Joseph P. Farrell

Pursuing his investigations of high financial fraud, international banking, hidden systems of finance, black budgets and breakaway civilizations, Farrell continues his examination of the post-war Nazi International, an "extra-territorial state" without borders or capitals, a network of terrorists, drug runners, and people in the very heights of financial power willing to commit financial fraud in amounts totaling trillions of dollars. Breakaway civilizations, black budgets, secret technology, international terrorism, giant corporate cartels, patent law and the hijacking of nature: Farrell explores 'the business model' of the post-war Axis elite.

364 Pages. 6x9 Paperback. Illustrated. $19.95. Code: TTW

ROSWELL AND THE REICH

The Nazi Connection

By Joseph P. Farrell

Farrell has meticulously reviewed the best-known Roswell research from UFO-ET advocates and skeptics alike, as well as some little-known source material, and comes to a radically different scenario of what happened in Roswell, New Mexico in July 1947, and why the US military has continued to cover it up to this day. Farrell presents a fascinating case sure to disturb both ET believers and disbelievers, namely, that what crashed may have been representative of an independent postwar Nazi power—an extraterritorial Reich monitoring its old enemy, America, and the continuing development of the very technologies confiscated from Germany at the end of the War.

540 pages. 6x9 Paperback. Illustrated. $19.95. Code: RWR

SECRETS OF THE UNIFIED FIELD

The Philadelphia Experiment, the Nazi Bell, and the Discarded Theory

by Joseph P. Farrell

Farrell examines the now discarded Unified Field Theory. American and German wartime scientists and engineers determined that, while the theory was incomplete, it could nevertheless be engineered. Chapters include: The Meanings of "Torsion"; Wringing an Aluminum Can; The Mistake in Unified Field Theories and Their Discarding by Contemporary Physics; Three Routes to the Doomsday Weapon: Quantum Potential, Torsion, and Vortices; Tesla's Meeting with FDR; Arnold Sommerfeld and Electromagnetic Radar Stealth; Electromagnetic Phase Conjugations, Phase Conjugate Mirrors, and Templates; The Unified Field Theory, the Torsion Tensor, and Igor Witkowski's Idea of the Plasma Focus; tons more.

340 pages. 6x9 Paperback. Illustrated. $18.95. Code: SOUF

NAZI INTERNATIONAL

The Nazi's Postwar Plan to Control Finance, Conflict, Physics and Space

by Joseph P. Farrell

Beginning with prewar corporate partnerships in the USA, including some with the Bush family, he moves on to the surrender of Nazi Germany, and evacuation plans of the Germans. He then covers the vast, and still-little-known recreation of Nazi Germany in South America with help of Juan Peron, I.G. Farben and Martin Bormann. Farrell then covers Nazi Germany's penetration of the Muslim world including Wilhelm Voss and Otto Skorzeny in Gamel Abdul Nasser's Egypt before moving on to the development and control of new energy technologies including the Bariloche Fusion Project, Dr. Philo Farnsworth's Plasmator, and the work of Dr. Nikolai Kozyrev. Finally, Farrell discusses the Nazi desire to control space, and examines their connection with NASA, the esoteric meaning of NASA Mission Patches.

412 pages. 6x9 Paperback. Illustrated. $19.95. Code: NZIN

ARKTOS

The Polar Myth in Science, Symbolism & Nazi Survival

by Joscelyn Godwin

Explored are the many tales of an ancient race said to have lived in the Arctic regions, such as Thule and Hyperborea. Progressing onward, he looks at modern polar legends: including the survival of Hitler, German bases in Antarctica, UFOs, the hollow earth, and the hidden kingdoms of Agartha and Shambala. Chapters include: Prologue in Hyperborea; The Golden Age; The Northern Lights; The Arctic Homeland; The Aryan Myth; The Thule Society; The Black Order; The Hidden Lands; Agartha and the Polaires; Shambhala; The Hole at the Pole; Antarctica; more.

220 Pages. 6x9 Paperback. Illustrated. Bib. Index. $16.95. Code: ARK

SAUCERS, SWASTIKAS AND PSYOPS
A History of a Breakaway Civilization
By Joseph P. Farrell

Farrell discusses SS Commando Otto Skorzeny; George Adamski; the alleged Hannebu and Vril craft of the Third Reich; The Strange Case of Dr. Hermann Oberth; Nazis in the US and their connections to "UFO contactees"; The Memes—an idea or behavior spread from person to person within a culture—are Implants. Chapters include: The Nov. 20, 1952 Contact: The Memes are Implants; The Interplanetary Federation of Brotherhood; Adamski's Technological Descriptions and Another ET Message: The Danger of Weaponized Gravity; Adamski's Retro-Looking Saucers, and the Nazi Saucer Myth; Dr. Oberth's 1968 Statements on UFOs and Extraterrestrials; more.

272 Pages. 6x9 Paperback. Illustrated. $19.95. Code: SSPY

LBJ AND THE CONSPIRACY TO KILL KENNEDY
By Joseph P. Farrell

Farrell says that a coalescence of interests in the military industrial complex, the CIA, and Lyndon Baines Johnson's powerful and corrupt political machine in Texas led to the events culminating in the assassination of JFK. Chapters include: Oswald, the FBI, and the CIA: Hoover's Concern of a Second Oswald; Oswald and the Anti-Castro Cubans; The Mafia; Hoover, Johnson, and the Mob; The FBI, the Secret Service, Hoover, and Johnson; The CIA and "Murder Incorporated"; Ruby's Bizarre Behavior; The French Connection and Permindex; Big Oil; The Dead Witnesses: Guy Bannister, Jr., Mary Pinchot Meyer, Rose Cheramie, Dorothy Killgallen, Congressman Hale Boggs; LBJ and the Planning of the Texas Trip; LBJ: A Study in Character, Connections, and Cabals; LBJ and the Aftermath: Accessory After the Fact; The Requirements of Coups D'État; more.

342 Pages. 6x9 Paperback. $19.95 Code: LCKK

THE TESLA PAPERS
Nikola Tesla on Free Energy & Wireless Transmission of Power
by Nikola Tesla, edited by David Hatcher Childress

David Hatcher Childress takes us into the incredible world of Nikola Tesla and his amazing inventions. Tesla's fantastic vision of the future, including wireless power, anti-gravity, free energy and highly advanced solar power. Also included are some of the papers, patents and material collected on Tesla at the Colorado Springs Tesla Symposiums, including papers on: •The Secret History of Wireless Transmission •Tesla and the Magnifying Transmitter •Design and Construction of a Half-Wave Tesla Coil •Electrostatics: A Key to Free Energy •Progress in Zero Point Energy Research •Electromagnetic Energy from Antennas to Atoms

325 Pages. 8x10 Paperback. Illustrated. $16.95. Code: TTP

COVERT WARS & THE CLASH OF CIVILIZATIONS
UFOs, Oligarchs and Space Secrecy
By Joseph P. Farrell

Farrell's customary meticulous research and sharp analysis blow the lid off of a worldwide web of nefarious financial and technological control that very few people even suspect exists. He elaborates on the advanced technology that they took with them at the "end" of World War II and shows how the breakaway civilizations have created a huge system of hidden finance with the involvement of various banks and financial institutions around the world. He investigates the current space secrecy that involves UFOs, suppressed technologies and the hidden oligarchs who control planet earth for their own gain and profit.

358 Pages. 6x9 Paperback. Illustrated. $19.95. Code: CWCC

HAUNEBU: THE SECRET FILES
The Greatest UFO Secret of All Time
By David Hatcher Childress

Childress brings us the incredible tale of the German flying disk known as the Haunebu. Although rumors of German flying disks have been around since the late years of WWII it was not until 1989 when a German researcher named Ralf Ettl living in London received an anonymous packet of photographs and documents concerning the planning and development of at least three types of unusual craft. Chapters include: A Saucer Full of Secrets; WWII as an Oil War; A Saucer Called Vril; Secret Cities of the Black Sun; The Strange World of Miguel Serrano; Set the Controls for the Heart of the Sun; Dark Side of the Moon: more. Includes a 16-page color section. Over 120 photographs and diagrams.

352 Pages. 6x9 Paperback. Illustrated. $22.00 Code: HBU

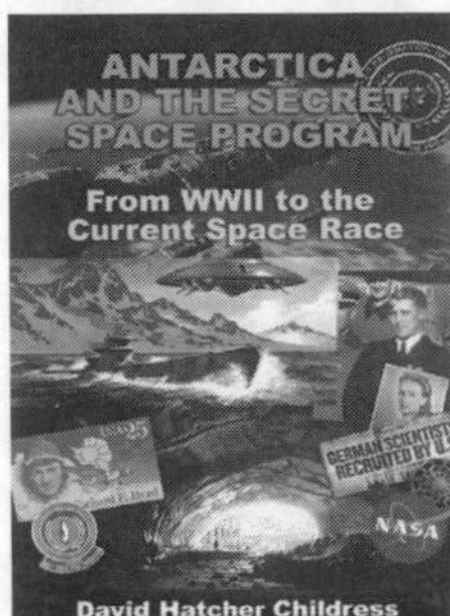

ANTARCTICA AND THE SECRET SPACE PROGRAM
Hatcher Childress

David Childress, popular author and star of the History Channel's show *Ancient Aliens*, brings us the incredible tale of Nazi submarines and secret weapons in Antarctica and elsewhere. He then examines Operation High-Jump with Admiral Richard Byrd in 1947 and the battle that he apparently had in Antarctica with flying saucers. Through "Operation Paperclip," the Nazis infiltrated aerospace companies, banking, media, and the US government, including NASA and the CIA after WWII. Does the US Navy have a secret space program that includes huge ships and hundreds of astronauts?

392 Pages. 6x9 Paperback. Illustrated. $22.00 Code: ASSP

THE ANTI-GRAVITY FILES
A Compilation of Patents and Reports
Edited by David Hatcher Childress

With plenty of technical drawings and explanations, this book reveals suppressed technology that will change the world in ways we can only dream of. Chapters include: A Brief History of Anti-Gravity Patents; The Motionless Electromagnet Generator Patent; Mercury Anti-Gravity Gyros; The Tesla Pyramid Engine; Anti-Gravity Propulsion Dynamics; The Machines in Flight; More Anti-Gravity Patents; Death Rays Anyone?; The Unified Field Theory of Gravity; and tons more. Heavily illustrated. 4-page color section.

216 pages. 8x10 Paperback. Illustrated. $22.00. Code: AGF

SECRET MARS: The Alien Connection
By M. J. Craig

While scientists spend billions of dollars confirming that microbes live in the Martian soil, people sitting at home on their computers studying the Mars images are making far more astounding discoveries… they have found the possible archaeological remains of an extraterrestrial civilization. Hard to believe? Well, this challenging book invites you to take a look at the astounding pictures yourself and make up your own mind. *Secret Mars* presents over 160 incredible images taken by American and European spacecraft that reveal possible evidence of a civilization that once lived, and may still live, on the planet Mars… powerful evidence that scientists are ignoring! A visual and fascinating book!

352 Pages. 6x9 Paperback. Illustrated. $19.95. Code: SMAR

THE GODS IN THE FIELDS

Michael, Mary and Alice-Guardians of Enchanted Britain

By Nigel Graddon

We learn of Britain's special place in the origins of ancient wisdom and of the "Sun-Men" who taught it to a humanity in its infancy. Aspects of these teachings are found all along the St. Michael ley: at Glastonbury, the location of Merlin and Arthur's Avalon; in the design and layout of the extraordinary Somerset Zodiac of which Glastonbury is a major part; in the amazing stone circles and serpentine avenues at Avebury and nearby Silbury Hill: portals to unimaginable worlds of mystery and enchantment; Chapters include: Michael, Mary and Merlin; England's West Country; The Glastonbury Zodiac; Wiltshire; The Gods in the Fields; Michael, Mary and Alice; East of the Line; Table of Michael and Mary Locations; more.

280 Pages. 6x9 Paperback. Illustrated. $19.95. Code: GIF

AXIS OF THE WORLD

The Search for the Oldest American Civilization

by Igor Witkowski

Polish author Witkowski's research reveals remnants of a high civilization that was able to exert its influence on almost the entire planet, and did so with full consciousness. Sites around South America show that this was not just one of the places influenced by this culture, but a place where they built their crowning achievements. Easter Island, in the southeastern Pacific, constitutes one of them. The Rongo-Rongo language that developed there points westward to the Indus Valley. Taken together, the facts presented by Witkowski provide a fresh, new proof that an antediluvian, great civilization flourished several millennia ago.

220 pages. 6x9 Paperback. Illustrated. $18.95. Code: AXOW

LEY LINE & EARTH ENERGIES

An Extraordinary Journey into the Earth's Natural Energy System

by David Cowan & Chris Arnold

The mysterious standing stones, burial grounds and stone circles that lace Europe, the British Isles and other areas have intrigued scientists, writers, artists and travellers through the centuries. How do ley lines work? How did our ancestors use Earth energy to map their sacred sites and burial grounds? How do ghosts and poltergeists interact with Earth energy? How can Earth spirals and black spots affect our health? This exploration shows how natural forces affect our behavior, how they can be used to enhance our health and well being.

368 pages. 6x9 Paperback. Illustrated. $18.95. Code: LLEE

THE BRINGER OF LIFE

A Cosmic History of the Divine Feminine

By Hayley A. Ramsey

Who and what is the divine feminine? What does She represent, and where can She be found? Hayley Ramsey starts at the beginning of time itself and explains the origins of goddess veneration and follows What caused the shift from matriarchal society to a patriarchal society? What was the relationship between religions such as Christianity and the suppression of the goddess? Ramsey examines the connections between Mary Magdalene, Jesus, and the Holy Grail while considering the importance of astrological precession. Many believe that She disappeared, but perhaps Her veneration went underground. Ramsey proposes the goddess and Her followers never disappeared, but instead She became shrouded in allegory and symbolism by different secret societies that still exist today. Is there a connection between the medieval Knights Templar, the divine feminine, and modern Freemasonry?

338 Pages. 6x9 Paperback. Illustrated. $18.95. Code: BOLF

ORDER FORM

10% Discount When You Order 3 or More Items!

One Adventure Place
P.O. Box 74
Kempton, Illinois 60946
United States of America
Tel.: 815-253-6390 • Fax: 815-253-6300
Email: auphq@frontiernet.net
http://www.adventuresunlimitedpress.com

ORDERING INSTRUCTIONS

- ✓ Remit by USD$ Check, Money Order or Credit Card
- ✓ Visa, Master Card, Discover & AmEx Accepted
- ✓ Paypal Payments Can Be Made To: info@wexclub.com
- ✓ Prices May Change Without Notice
- ✓ 10% Discount for 3 or More Items

SHIPPING CHARGES

United States

- ✓ POSTAL BOOK RATE
- ✓ Postal Book Rate { $5.00 First Item; 50¢ Each Additional Item
- ✓ Priority Mail { $8.50 First Item; $2.00 Each Additional Item
- ✓ UPS { $9.00 First Item (Minimum 5 Books); $1.50 Each Additional Item

NOTE: UPS Delivery Available to Mainland USA Only

Canada

- ✓ Postal Air Mail { $19.00 First Item; $3.00 Each Additional Item
- ✓ Personal Checks or Bank Drafts MUST BE US$ and Drawn on a US Bank
- ✓ Canadian Postal Money Orders OK
- ✓ Payment MUST BE US$

All Other Countries

- ✓ Sorry, No Surface Delivery!
- ✓ Postal Air Mail { $29.00 First Item; $7.00 Each Additional Item
- ✓ Checks and Money Orders MUST BE US$ and Drawn on a US Bank or branch.
- ✓ Paypal Payments Can Be Made in US$ To: info@wexclub.com

SPECIAL NOTES

- ✓ RETAILERS: Standard Discounts Available
- ✓ BACKORDERS: We Backorder all Out-of-Stock Items Unless Otherwise Requested
- ✓ PRO FORMA INVOICES: Available on Request
- ✓ DVD Return Policy: Replace defective DVDs only

ORDER ONLINE AT: www.adventuresunlimitedpress.com

10% Discount When You Order 3 or More Items!

Please check: ✓

☐ This is my first order ☐ I have ordered before

Name

Address

City

State/Province | Postal Code

Country

Phone: Day | Evening

Fax | Email

Item Code	Item Description	Qty	Total

Please check: ✓

☐ Postal-Surface

☐ Postal-Air Mail (Priority in USA)

☐ UPS (Mainland USA only)

Subtotal ▸

Less Discount-10% for 3 or more items ▸

Balance ▸

Illinois Residents 6.25% Sales Tax ▸

Previous Credit ▸

Shipping ▸

Total (check/MO in USD$ only) ▸

☐ Visa/MasterCard/Discover/American Express

Card Number:

Expiration Date: Security Code:

✓ SEND A CATALOG TO A FRIEND: